ST. ATHANASIUS

THE LIFE
OF SAINT ANTONY

Ancient Christian Writers

THE WORKS OF THE FATHERS IN TRANSLATION

EDITED BY

JOHANNES QUASTEN, S. T. D.
*Professor of Ancient Church History
and Christian Archaeology*

JOSEPH C. PLUMPE, Ph. D.
*Professor of Patristic Greek
and Ecclesiastical Latin*

The Catholic University of America
Washington, D. C.

No. 10

ST. ATHANASIUS

THE LIFE
OF SAINT ANTONY

NEWLY TRANSLATED AND ANNOTATED

BY

ROBERT T. MEYER, Ph. D.

Assistant Professor of Comparative Philology
Catholic University of America
Washington, D. C.

NEWMAN PRESS

New York, N.Y. / Mahwah, N.J.

Nihil Obstat:

Johannes Quasten, S.T.D.
Censor Deputatus

Imprimatur:

Patricius A. O'Boyle, D.D.
Archiepiscopus Washingtonensis
die 7 Martii 1950

Library of Congress
Catalog Card Number: 78-62454

ISBN: 0-8091-0250-1

PUBLISHED BY PAULIST PRESS
997 Macarthur Boulevard
Mahwah, New Jersey 07430

PRINTED AND BOUND IN THE UNITED STATES OF AMERICA

CONTENTS

ST. ATHANASIUS

THE LIFE
OF SAINT ANTONY

INTRODUCTION

The present volume contains the most important document of early monasticism, *The Life of St. Antony*, whose author is no less a man than the great St. Athanasius himself.

Antony, generally considered the father of Christian monachism or monasticism,[1] was born about the year 250 of well-to-do parents in Middle Egypt. If Sozomen's information is not confused, his home town was Coma.[2] His parents were Christians. Athanasius stresses that the boy was attached to them and to home life, finding school and companionship with other children distasteful.

He was eighteen or twenty years of age when his parents died, leaving him guardian of his younger and only sister. One day, about six months later, he happened to enter the church when he was struck by the reading of the Gospel in which the Lord speaks to the rich young man: *If thou wilt be perfect, go sell all that thou hast, and give it to the poor; and come, follow me and thou shalt have treasure in Heaven.*[3] Applying this to himself, he went home and distributed his land—a fertile farm of more than two hundred acres—among the townspeople. He sold all his other belongings. He did not wish the goods of the world to hamper himself or his sister, and so he also disposed of the money received, giving it to the poor. Only a small sum was retained for his sister.

But once again as he went to church, he was moved by a lesson of the Gospel: *Be not solicitous for the morrow.*[4]

3

Taking this as another gesture from on high, he distributed the remaining fund to the poor. Placing his sister in the care of a community of pious women, he began to practice the ascetic life near his old home. At this time such life was not yet practiced in common, but one who desired to lead the perfect life went apart from the rest, and apart from any organization practiced it by himself. Near Antony's native village there lived an old man who had given himself to a life of asceticism from his youth. Drawn by his example, Antony left his home surroundings and observed carefully the ascetic practices of this solitary and of other men like him. He endeavored to imitate the special virtue of each, not in a spirit of pride or contention, but with the purpose of becoming a model ascetic in the eyes of God. Prayer was combined with fasting and manual labor, for his teachers in the ascetic life agreed with the Apostle who said that *he that is lazy, neither let him eat.*[5]

Later he departed to some tombs that lay at a considerable distance from the village. An obliging friend locked him in an empty vault and brought him bread from time to time. Athanasius reports (10) that Antony remained here until he was approximately thirty-five years of age,[6] in his solitude fighting off the temptations of the flesh and the attacks of demons. Because of his constancy the Lord promised him in a vision that He would be ever at his side in time of trial and make him renowned throughout the world. He left this retreat to move to the right side of the Nile to the "Outer Mountain" [7] at Pispir, where he occupied a deserted fort.

After living in his new solitude for a long time—St.

Athanasius states (14) that this period lasted twenty years
—he was visited by friends who wished to copy his holy
life. They broke down the door of his retreat, and Antony
emerged, fresh and unchanged, and performing miracles
and preaching the love of Christ. Many gathered around
him to follow the ascetic life. He became their leader,
teaching them constantly by word and example, fostering
their zeal, and attracting still others to the ascetic life.
From this period we have a long discourse (16-43) delivered by Antony on the vocation of the monk, the temptations of Satan and his powerlessness in the presence of
recourse to prayer against him, and the gift, coming from
the Holy Spirit, of discerning good and evil spirits.

At about this time we also find Antony at the head of
a group of monks going to Alexandria during the persecution of Maximin Daja. His purpose was to offer himself
for martyrdom, if the Lord willed it. He spent his time
"ministering to the confessors in the mines and in the
prisons." [8] But to his grief it did not please God that he
should die a martyr, and when the persecution had ended,
he returned to his cell, to be a "daily martyr to his conscience, ever fighting the battles of the faith" (47).

While Antony was the recognized superior of the monks·
who had subjected themselves to him, he remained ever
true to his eremitic vocation. He needed to be alone; and
to be alone, he left Pispir and travelled for some days
through the desert towards the Red Sea. When he had
found a spring and some date palms, he settled there at
the foot of a mountain. This was the "Inner Mountain," [9]
still known as Dêr Mar Antonios, where he cultivated a
small garden and spent his time in prayer and meditation.

Charles Kingsley has this to say of Antony's new retreat:

The eastward view from Antony's old home must be one of the most glorious in the world, save for the want of verdure and of life. For Antony, as he looked across the Gulf of Akaba, across which, far above, the Israelites had passed in old times, could see the sacred peaks of Sinai, flaming against the blue sky with that intensity of hue which is scarcely exaggerated, it is said, by the bright scarlet color in which Sinai is always painted in medieval illuminations.[10]

From this retreat he was to make quite regular trips to visit and counsel his spiritual subjects.

And other recorded facts, too, show that Antony must not be thought of as one who immersed himself in his ascetic practices and the eremitical life to the exclusion of all else. Athanasius pictures him as going to Alexandria and publicly denouncing the Arian heretics and "Christ-fighters" (68-70). He did not refuse to enter discussion with the "Greeks," the followers of Neo-Platonic thought (72-80). The world beat a path to his cell in the heart of the desert, seeking cures of body and mind and soul; and, as they had done at Pispir, monks came to him for his sympathy and practical advice.

When he felt his end approaching, he wished to die alone on his mountain—the "Inner Mountain"—where he had spent so many decades of "daily martyrdom." After a brief farewell to the brethren on the "Outer Mountain," he went back to his retreat in the company of two monks, Macarius and Amatas, who lived with him because of his advanced age. He then made his last will and testament: his place of burial was never to be revealed by the two monks; further, to Bishop Athanasius he left a sheepskin and a cloak, gifts which he had once received from him; Bishop Serapion was to receive his other sheepskin, but they were to keep the hair shirt for themselves (91). With a final blessing for them, he gave up his spirit.

When Antony died in the year 356 at the age of one hundred and five years, he was the recognized founder and father of monasticism. His original settlement at Pispir of monks who looked to him as their superior, had become the center of the solitary life in Egypt.[11] It was a school for asceticism, including such famous solitaries as Hilarion, who visited Antony in his youth and later helped spread the monastic life in Palestine;[12] Macarius the Elder,[13] spiritual father to several thousand monks in the desert of Scete; Amoun,[14] the founder of Nitrian monasticism; Paul the Simple, and others. As Dom Cuthbert Butler has said:

Whether in works which may claim to be history, or in the vaguer traditions enshrined in the *Apophthegmata,* or in the pure romances, a firmly set tradition ever looks back to Antony as the inspirer, nay even the creator, of that monastic system, which . . . had by the year 370 attained to vast proportions in Egypt and elsewhere.[15]

For the history of Egyptian monasticism during the fourth and fifth centuries we are dependent upon Palladius' celebrated record of monastic biographies known as *The Lausiac History,* and the various collections, in many versions, of "Sayings of the Fathers" (or Elders), called *Apophthegmata Patrum* or *Verba Seniorum.* We should also mention, among others, a third source, the anonymous *Historia Monachorum in Aegypto (History of the Monks in Egypt),* long thought to be an original work in Latin by Rufinus. The solution in great part of the baffling problems and riddles presented by this mass of literature was achieved by some of the most brilliant research

of recent times and is to be credited principally to the
English Benedictine just mentioned, Dom Cuthbert Butler,
and the German scholar, Wilhelm Bousset.[16] The constant recurrence of references to Antony and his teachings
and to incidents in his life [17] indicates the high esteem in
which his memory was held. If we were limited to these
general works of monastic lives and traditions, we should
have a very high opinion of the position he held in the
development of monasticism in Egypt.

But it is fortunate, and also important for the development of monasticism in the West, that St. Athanasius
turned his attention to writing a biography of Antony as
early as 357, within a year after his death. The year 357
is generally accepted today as the date of composition of
the *Vita*,[18] though the view of the Maurist editors that it
was written at a later date, in the year 365, still finds·
support.[19] But modern criticism has concerned itself with
the authenticity of the biography rather than the date of
composition.[20]

The contemporaries or near-contemporaries of St.
Athanasius never hesitated to ascribe the authorship to
him. In 392 St. Jerome shows that he was acquainted with
the *Vita*, both in the original and in the Latin version
made of it by Evagrius [21] approximately thirty years
earlier. St. Gregory Nazianzen remarks that Athanasius
wrote a life of St. Antony in the form of a narrative.[22]
Further, the Herodotus of the desert Fathers, Palladius,
quotes an incident recorded in the life of the Nitrian monk
Amoun and indicates his source, "The blessed Athanasius
the bishop in his life of Antony." [23]

"Since the Reformation the general tendency of protes-
tant writers has been to discredit, of Roman Catholics

to maintain the authority of the *Vita*." This statement by an eminent editor of the writings of St. Athanasius, Archibald Robertson, held quite true when it was written nearly sixty years ago.[24] Among the Reformers attacking the authenticity were the Magdeburg Centuriators, the Calvinist theologian Andrew Rivet, and the ex-Premonstratensian Casimir Oudin; on the Catholic side as defending the Athanasian authorship the names of Bellarmin and Montfaucon were the most conspicuous. In modern times the last serious attempt to deny the genuineness of the *Vita* was made some seventy years ago by the Breslau professor H. Weingarten.[25] Today no one denies that St. Athanasius is the author, and its unique importance not only for the development of monasticism, but for monasticism's earliest history is generally conceded.

One of the difficulties urged against the authority of the *Vita* also strikes the modern reader: the long passages representing discourses by Antony and setting forth a high degree of learning—on the theory of asceticism (16-43), on Greek philosophy, especially Neo-Platonism (72-80), and against Arianism (69). Against this it was urged that Athanasius states or intimates in several places in the *Life* that Antony possessed no book learning. It is even doubtful that he could read or write.[26] The most we can say regarding these sections is that they are both Antony and Athanasius: equidem quid Antonio quid Athanasio tribuendum sit, vix diiudicari posse concedo—as the learned critic of Weingarten put it.[27]

Athanasius meets rather well the requirements of modern historical criticism as far as the sources of his information go.[28] He had himself known Antony well, having spent part of his youth with him, probably before he was ordained deacon in 318. Antony had visited him in Alexandria (71), and Athanasius had probably spent some time with him in the desert during one of his periods of exile. Further, the author indicates near the close of the Prologue that he has profited from information given him by one "who was his (Antony's) companion over a long period." [29]

If we accept the heading preserved in the ancient Latin version of Evagrius, the Prologue is addressed to monks in foreign parts—*ad peregrinos fratres*. This must refer to monks in the West who had apparently asked Athanasius to give some account of the life of Antony for their emulation. Athanasius had, of course, spent some time in the West on two different occasions, while exiled from Alexandria. His first stay was at Trier on the banks of the Mosel in 336-337.[30] The Eusebians forced him into exile a second time, and in March, 340, he set out for Rome.[31] Although in the following year he was exonerated by a Roman synod under Pope Julius, it was more than six years before he was free to return to the see of Alexandria. In the course of this stay he also came to Milan˙and revisited Trier. He had gone to Rome accompanied by a Nitric monk named Isidore. Palladius relates [32] how the monk became known to the Roman senate and the Roman noblewomen; and we have it on the authority of St. Jerome [33] that at this time Roman society became acquainted with the life of St. Antony and cherished admiration for the monastic life. The part played by St. Athanasius in introducing monasticism to the West is most significant.[34]

For his own part Athanasius was anxious to perpetuate the memory of his friend and teacher in the ascetic life.

We must not, however, judge the *Vita* as we should a modern biography. We should expect him to press into service, as he did in his apologetic works, his earlier rhetorical training in the schools of Alexandria. For his purposes he found in the classical Greek literature the literary type known as the *encomium,* exemplified by the *Agesilaus* of Xenophon, which itself harks back to the earlier *Evagoras* of Isocrates, long studied in the schools and used as a model by the rhetoricians.[35]

Formally, it may be said, the *Vita* composed by St. Athanasius is an *encomium* [36] in that it gives us Antony's nationality, parentage, education, and youth, and enumerates his good qualities. However, the likeness ends here in that the ancient *encomium* had as its purpose the praise of an important figure in public life, and hence placed much emphasis upon his personal achievements, especially in the service of the state. Xenophon greatly admired the heroic Agesilaus for his deeds and his ideal Spartan character—he saw in him the ideal of a good king.[37] Athanasius saw in Antony the ideal monk and wished to leave behind a literary monument to perpetuate his memory and to serve as a model for others, notably for such as sought perfection in the monastic life.

Modern critics have been quick to find another kind of literary model of the *Vita S. Antoni* in the *vitae* of certain philosophers.[38] Philostratus had written a biography of Apollonius of Tyana, Iamblichus—among others—wrote one of Pythagoras, and Porphyry composed a life of his teacher Plotinus. These biographical works portray the ideal philosophical sage in all his virtues and contain graphic accounts of the extraordinary deeds performed by the philosophers to prove their claim of occult knowledge

to their followers. St. Athanasius' *Antony,* it must be
owned, contains a number of striking parallels to the life
history given by Porphyry of his master. It may indeed be,
as List is inclined to think,[39] that St. Athanasius was con-
scious of Porphyry's biography as he wrote the life of his
desert hero, of the "unlettered" Antony who had not
sought the fame of worldly knowledge and wisdom, who
yet was sought out and respected by philosophers, among
them followers of Plotinus, who laid claim to such worldly
accomplishments. If any such tendency, of showing his
hero superior to that of Porphyry, was in the mind of
Athanasius, he certainly succeeded in that purpose,[40]
though it was a very secondary one with him.

At any rate, besides the ancient classical models of biography, the newer type must have been known to Athanasius—that of the sage or the mystic, who drew great
crowds of followers, not on the battlefield or in the affairs
of state, but in the equally dramatic battle with self and
the forces of nature. However this literary tradition may
have served the inspiration and composition of Athanasius, he—consciously or unconsciously—inaugurated a
third type of life story, the Christian biography. His hero,
Antony,. gains greatness not from the greatness of his
deeds or his wisdom, but from the monumental greatness
of his simplicity; from "uniting in himself in perfect harmony—renunciation and generosity, the love of solitude
and the love of man, independence and humility"; [41] from
his great love of the Faith, his great love of the Church,
his great mystical love of God. The ancient ideal type,
the *hero* in the natural order, or later, the *sage* in the
intellectual order, is here superseded by the *saint* in the
supernatural order. The highest prototype of classical

antiquity, the *pius Aeneas,* was but a pale ghost beside
Saint Antony who achieved what Socrates and Plato and
Plotinus could only grope for in their highest speculation.
The crowning achievement of Athanasius is that he com-
bined the ancient literary forms of biography with the
Christian element, and produced a type that was to in-
fluence all subsequent Greek and Latin hagiography.

There is a striking popular element in the *Vita*—the
accounts of demons. While it is true that such material is
less overwrought and less obstrusive than in many subsequent accounts of the lives of monks, still we sense that
there is quite too much of it in the *Vita*: besides all the
incidents of violent and strange encounters with Satan and
his helpers, the long address (16-43) which Antony is
shown as giving to his fellow monks and which takes up
nearly one-fourth of the entire work, is almost in its en-
tirety a discourse on demonology.[42]

No single or complete explanation of the great stress on
this phenomenon is possible. Many factors enter here—
the ancient inability to account for certain natural causes;
the Christian conviction that the pagan gods and idols
were in reality demons and that they plagued especially
the Christians because Christianity was destroying more
and more their dominance of the world; Gnostic traditions; certain occult influences which may have been more
pronounced in antiquity than now and which we cannot
quite explain even now; Athanasius' tendency to empha-
size and aggrandize the heroic in his hero; his purpose to
edify and to instruct his addressees—other monks and
ascetics; the influence of similar accounts in other Christian literature, notably the popular "acts of martyrdom"
(acta martyrum).[43] Allowing that these and other con-

siderations may fall short of explaining satisfactorily the role that demons play in Antony's life story, careful reading of his experiences and counsels also reveals many sane and acute observations made by him in the realm of the psychological and of the spiritual life.[44]

The *Life of St. Antony* enjoyed a tremendous popularity in ancient times and through the Middle Ages. It was read in faraway Gaul less than twenty years after it was written.[45] Probably at the instance of St. Jerome,[46] Evagrius translated or paraphrased it into Latin while he was still a presbyter, about the year 370. It served as the literary forerunner of Jerome's lives of Paul and Hilarion. St. Augustine tells us in the *Confessions* that it was one of the deciding influences in his own conversion.[47] Ponticianus, who recounted the life of Antony to him, probably had it in the Latin version of Evagrius.[48] In fact, as time went on, the Evagrian version enjoyed an existence and fame quite apart from the Greek original. Later, in the thirteenth century, it was incorporated, in somewhat abbreviated form, into the *Legenda Aurea* of Jacobus de Voragine. In succeeding centuries this edition of it served as the source of many vernacular translations in Western Europe. Further, it was largely through this medium that the story of St. Antony kindled the inspiration of artists.[49] Sculptors and painters have represented numerous scenes from the *Life of St. Antony* in wood and metal, in oils and stained glass.[50] The temptation of St. Antony particularly recommended itself to artistic treatment, allowing as it did, free scope to the imagination. In more recent times it provided Flaubert with the title to one of his works.

Again, a Syriac version of the *Vita* was made very early, perhaps as early as the Latin by Evagrius.[51]

, , ,

The Greek text of the *Vita S. Antoni* which appeared in the celebrated Benedictine edition by Bernard de Montfaucon in Paris, 1698, has never been superseded. This as reprinted in Migne's *Patrologia Graeca* 26 (1887) 835-976 (published separately by A. F. Maunoury, Paris 1887, 1890), has served as the text for the present translation. The following modern translations have also been consulted:

Clarus, L., *Das Leben des heiligen Antonius von Athanasius dem Grossen* (Münster i. W. 1857).

Ellershaw, H., *Life of Antony*, in *Select Writings and Letters of Athanasius, Bishop of Alexandria*, edited by A. Robertson (A Select Library of Nicene and Post-Nicene Fathers of the Christian Church, Second Series 4, New York-Oxford-London 1892) 195-221.

Lavaud, B., *Antoine le Grand, père des moines. Sa vie par saint Athanase et autres textes* (Lyon 1943).

McLaughlin, Dom J. B., *St. Antony the Hermit by St. Athanasius* (New York 1924).

Mertel, H., *Des heiligen Athanasius Leben des heiligen Antonius*, in *Des heiligen Athanasius ausgewählte Schriften* 2 (Bibliothek der Kirchenväter 31, Munich 1917) 676-777.[52]

PROLOGUE

ATHANASIUS THE BISHOP TO THE
BRETHREN IN FOREIGN PARTS [1]

The rivalry you have entered on with the monks in Egypt is excellent, determined as you are to equal or even to surpass them in your practice of the ascetic life. In fact, by now there are monasteries in your country too and the name of "monk" has established itself. This your purpose is praiseworthy indeed, and may your prayers prevail upon God to fulfill it!

Now, you have also asked me for an account of the life of the blessed Antony: you would like to learn how he came to practice asceticism, what he was previous to this, what his death was like, and whether everything said about him is true. You have in mind to model your lives after his life of zeal. I am very happy to accede to your request, for I, too, derive real profit and help from the mere recollection of Antony; [2] and I feel that you also, once you have heard the story, will not merely admire the man but will wish to emulate his resolution as well. Really, for monks the life of Antony is an ideal pattern of the ascetical life.

So, do not disbelieve the reports you have received from others concerning him, but be assured that you have heard very little from them. Indeed, they have scarcely told you all when there is so much to tell; and when I, too, whatever I may convey to you by letter at your request, shall be giving you only a few of the recollections I have of him. You on your part must not cease to make enquiries of all voyagers arriving from here. Thus perhaps as each tells what he knows, an account will be had that does approximate justice to him.[3]

Well, when I received your letter I wanted to send for some of the monks, especially those who used to associate with him most closely. Thus I might have learned additional details and sent you a fuller account. But the sailing season is about over and the postman is growing impatient; therefore, I make haste to write to Your Reverence what I myself know—for I have seen him often—and whatever I was able to learn from him who was his companion over a long period and poured water on his hands.[4] Throughout I have been scrupulously considerate of the truth: I wanted no one to refuse credence because what he heard was too much, nor, again, to make light of the man because he did not learn enough about him.

BIRTH AND YOUTH OF ANTONY

1. Antony was an Egyptian by birth.[5] His parents were of good stock and well-to-do; and because they were Christians he himself was brought up a Christian. As a child he lived with his parents, knowing nothing but them and his home; and when he grew to be a boy and was advancing in age, he did not take to schooling,[6] desiring to shun even the companionship of other children: his one desire was, as the Scripture states concerning Jacob,[7] to lead a simple life at home. Of course, he attended church [8] with his parents; and here he did not show the disinterest

of a child nor youth's contempt for such things. No, obeying his parents, he paid attention to the lessons that were read, and carefully kept in his heart the profit he gleaned from them. Again, notwithstanding the easy circumstances in which he lived as a boy, he never importuned his parents for fancy and rich food, nor did he take any pleasure in such. He was satisfied with what was put before him, and asked no more.

ANTONY'S CALL AND HIS FIRST
STEPS IN ASCETICISM

2. Upon his parents' death he was left alone with an only sister who was very young. He was about eighteen or twenty years old at the time and took care of the house and his sister. Less than six months had passed since his parents' death when, as usual, he chanced to be on his way to church. As he was walking along, he collected his thoughts and reflected how the Apostles left everything and followed the Savior; [9] also how the people in Acts sold what they had and laid it at the feet of the Apostles for distribution among the needy; [10] and what great hope is laid up in Heaven for such as these.[11] With these thoughts in his mind he entered the church. And it so happened that the Gospel was being read at that moment and he heard the passage in which the Lord says to the rich man: *If thou wilt be perfect, go sell all that thou hast, and give it to the poor; and come, follow me and thou shalt have treasure in Heaven.*[12] As though God had put him in mind of the saints and as though the reading had been directed especially to him,[13] Antony immediately left the

church and gave to the townspeople the property he had from his forebears—three hundred *arurae*,[14] very fertile and beautiful to see. He did not want it to encumber himself or his sister in any way whatever. He sold all the rest, the chattels they had, and gave the tidy sum he received to the poor, keeping back only a little for his sister.

3. But once again as he entered the church, he heard the Lord saying in the Gospel: *Be not solicitous for the morrow.*[15] He could not bear to wait longer, but went out and distributed those things also to the poor.[16] His sister he placed with known and trusted virgins, giving her to the nuns [17] to be brought up. Then he himself devoted all his time to ascetic living, intent on himself and living a life of self-denial, near his own house. For there were not yet so many monasteries in Egypt, and no monk even knew of the faraway desert. Whoever wished to concern himself with his own destiny practiced asceticism by himself not far from his own village.

Now, at that time there was in the next village an old man who had lived the ascetic life in solitude from his youth. When Antony saw him, he was *zealous for that which is good;* [18] and he promptly began to stay in the vicinity of the town. Then, if he heard of a zealous soul anywhere, like a wise bee he left to search him out, nor did he return home before he had seen him; and only when he had received from him, as it were, provisions for his journey to virtue, did he go back.

There, then, he spent the time of his initiation and made good his determination not to return to the house of his fathers nor to think about his relatives, but to devote all his affections and all his energy to the continued prac-

tice of the ascetic life. He did manual labor,[19] for he had
heard that *he that is lazy, neither let him eat.*[20] Some of
his earnings he spent for bread and some he gave to the
poor. He prayed constantly, having learnt that we must
pray in private [21] without cease.[22] Again, he was so atten-
tive at the reading of the Scripture lessons that nothing
escaped him: he retained everything [23] and so his memory
served him in place of books.

4. Thus lived Antony and he was loved by all. He, in
turn, subjected himself in all sincerity to the pious men
whom he visited and made it his endeavor to learn for his
own benefit just how each was superior to him in zeal and
ascetic practice.[24] He observed the graciousness of one, the
earnestness at prayer in another; studied the even temper
of one and the kindheartedness of another; fixed his
attention on the vigils kept by one and on the studies
pursued by another; admired one for his patient endur-
ance, another for his fasting and sleeping on the ground;
watched closely this man's meekness and the forbearance
shown by another; and in one and all alike he marked
especially devotion to Christ and the love they had for one
another.[25]

Having thus taken his fill, he would return to his own
place of asceticism. Then he assimilated in himself what
he had obtained from each and devoted all his energies to
realizing in himself the virtues of all.[26] Moreover, he had
no quarrels with anyone of his own age, excepting this
that he would not be second to them in the better things;
and this he did in such a way that no one was hurt in his
feelings, but they, too, rejoiced on his account. And so all
the villagers and the good men with whom he associated

saw what kind of a man he was and they called him "God's Friend"; and they were fond of him as a son or as a brother.

EARLY CONFLICTS WITH DEMONS

5. But the Devil, the hater and envier of good,[27] could not bear to see such resolution in a young man, but set about employing his customary tactics also against him.[28] First, he tried to make him desert the ascetic life by putting him in mind of his property, the care of his sister, the attachments of kindred, the love of money, the love of fame, the myriad pleasures of eating, and all the other amenities of life. Finally, he represented to him the austerity and all the toil that go with virtue, suggesting that the body is weak and time is long. In short, he raised up in his mind a great dust cloud of arguments, intending to make him abandon his set purpose.

The Enemy saw, however, that he was powerless in the face of Antony's determination and that it was rather he who was being bested because of the man's steadfastness and vanquished by his solid faith and routed by Antony's constant prayer. He then put his trust in the weapons that are *in the navel of his own belly*.[29] Priding himself in these—for they are his choice snare against the young— he advanced to attack the young man, troubling him so by night and harassing him by day, that even those who saw Antony could perceive the struggle going on between the two. The Enemy would suggest filthy thoughts, but the other would dissipate them by his prayers; he would try to incite him to lust, but Antony, sensing shame, would gird his body with his faith, with his prayers and his fasting. The wretched Devil even dared to masquerade as a woman by night and to impersonate such in every possible way, merely in order to deceive Antony. But he filled his thoughts with Christ and reflected upon the nobility of the soul that comes from Him, and its spirituality, and thus quenched the glowing coal of temptation. And again the Enemy suggested pleasure's seductive charm. But Antony, angered, of course, and grieved, kept his thoughts upon the threat of fire and the pain of the worm.[30] Holding these up as his shield, he came through unscathed.

The entire experience put the Enemy to shame. Indeed, he who had thought he was like to God,[31] was here made a fool of by a stripling of a man. He who in his conceit disdained flesh and blood, was now routed by a man in the flesh. Verily, the Lord worked with this man—He who for our sakes took on flesh [32] and gave to his body victory over the Devil. Thus all who fight in earnest can say: *Not I, but the grace of God with me.*[33]

6. Finally when the dragon could not conquer Antony by this last means either, but saw himself thrust out of his heart, gnashing his teeth, as Scripture says,[34] he changed his person, so to speak. As he is in his heart, precisely so did he appear to him—as a black boy; [35] and as though cringing to him, he no longer assailed him with thoughts —for he had been ousted, the imposter—but now using a human voice, he said: "Many a man have I deceived and very many have I overthrown; but now when I attacked you and your efforts as I have done with many others, I proved too weak."

"Who are you who speak thus to me?" Antony asked.

The other was quick to reply with whining voice: "I am the lover of fornication. It is my commission to waylay the youth and seduce them to this, and I am called the spirit of fornication. How many have I not deceived who were determined to keep their senses! How many chaste persons have I not seduced by my cajoleries! Incidentally, I am the one on whose account the Prophet reproaches the fallen, saying: *You were deceived by the spirit of fornication.*[36] Yes, it was I that tripped them up. I am the one who gave you so much trouble and as often was vanquished by you."

Antony then gave thanks to the Lord and taking courage against him, said: "Well then, you are quite despicable; you are black in your soul and you are as weak as a child. For the future you cause me no worry at all, for *the Lord is my helper and I will despise my enemies.*"[37] Hearing this, the Black One fled at once, cowering at his words and fearing to even come near the man.

7. This was Antony's first victory over the Devil; rather, let me say that this singular success in Antony was the Savior's, who *condemned sin in the flesh that the justification of the law might be fulfilled in us who walk not according to the flesh, but according to the spirit.*[38] Now, Antony did not grow careless and take too much for granted with himself, merely because the demon had been brought to his knees; nor did the Enemy, worsted as he was in the conflict, cease to lie in wait for him. He kept going around again like a lion [39] seeking a chance against him. But Antony, having learned from the Scriptures that the wiles of the Evil One are manifold,[40] practiced asceticism in earnest, bearing in mind that even if he could not

beguile his heart by pleasure of the body, he would certainly try to ensnare him by some other method; for the demon's love is sin. So he more and more mortified his body and brought it into subjection, lest having conquered on one occasion, he should be the loser on another.[41] He resolved, therefore, to accustom himself to a more austere way of life. And many marvelled at him, but he bore the life easily. The zeal that had pervaded his soul over a long time, had effected a good frame of mind in him, with the result that even a slight inspiration received from others caused him to respond with great enthusiasm. For instance, he kept nocturnal vigil with such determination that he often spent the entire night sleepless, and this not only once, but many times to their admiration. Again, he ate but once a day, after sunset; indeed, sometimes only every other day, and frequently only every fourth day did he partake of food. His food was bread and salt; his drink, water only. Meat and wine we need not even mention, for no such thing could be found with the other ascetics either. He was content to sleep on a rush mat, though as a rule he lay down on the bare ground. He deprecated the use of oil for the skin, saying that young men should practice asceticism in real earnest and not go for the things that enervate the body; rather they should accustom it to hard work, bearing in mind the words of the Apostle: *When I am weak, then am I powerful.*[42] It was a dictum of his that the soul's energy thrives when the body's desires are feeblest.

He further held to the following truly remarkable conviction: he thought he should appraise his progress in virtue and his consequent withdrawal from the world not by any length of time spent in them, but by his attachment and devotion to them. Accordingly, he gave no thought to the passage of time, but day by day, as though he were just beginning the ascetic life, he made greater effort toward perfection. He kept repeating to himself the words of Paul: *Forgetting the things that are behind, and reaching out to the things that are before,*[43] remembering, too, the voice of Elias the Prophet saying: *The Lord liveth, in whose sight I stand this day.*[44] He observed that when he said "*this* day," he was not counting the time that was past, but as though constantly beginning anew, he worked hard each day to make of himself such as one should be to appear before God—pure of heart and ready to follow His will and none other. And he used to say to himself that the life led by the great Elias should serve the ascetic as a mirror in which always to study his own life.

ANTONY'S LIFE IN THE TOMBS. FURTHER STRUGGLES WITH DEMONS

8. So did Antony master himself. Then he left for the tombs which lay at some distance from the village. He had requested one of his acquaintances to bring him bread at long intervals. He then entered one of the tombs, the man mentioned locked the door on him, and he remained alone within. This was too much for the Enemy to bear, indeed, he feared that presently he would fill the desert too with his asceticism. So he came one night with a great number of demons and lashed him so unmercifully that he lay on the ground speechless from the pain. He maintained that the pain was so severe that the blows could not have

been inflicted by any man and cause such agony. By
God's Providence—for the Lord does not overlook those
who hope in Him—his acquaintance came by next day
with the bread for him. When he opened the door and
saw him lying on the ground as though dead, he lifted him
up and carried him to the village church and laid him
upon the floor. Many of his kinsfolk and the people from
the village sat around Antony as round a corpse. But
about midnight he regained consciousness and awoke.
When he saw that all were asleep and that his friend alone
was awake, he beckoned him to his side and asked him to
lift him up again and carry him back to the tombs without waking anyone.

9. So the man carried him back and the door was
locked as before and once more he was alone within. Because of the blows received he was too feeble to stand, so
he prayed lying down. His prayer finished, he called out
with a shout: "Here am I, Antony. I am not cowed by
your blows, and even though you should give me more,
nothing shall separate me from the love of Christ." [46]
Then he began to sing: *If camps shall stand against me,
my heart shall not fear.*[47]

So thought and spoke the ascetic, but the hater of good,
the Enemy, marvelled that after all the blows he had the
courage to come back, called together his dogs,[48] and
bursting with rage, said: "You see that I have not
stopped this fellow, neither by the spirit of fornication
nor by blows; on the contrary, he even challenges us.
Let us go after him in another way."

Well, the role of an evildoer is easy for the Devil. That
night, therefore, they made such a din that the whole

place seemed to be shaken by an earthquake. It was as
though demons were breaking through the four walls of
the little chamber and bursting through them in the forms
of beasts and reptiles. All at once the place was filled with
the phantoms of lions, bears, leopards, bulls, and of serpents, asps, and scorpions, and of wolves; and each moved
according to the shape it had assumed. The lion roared,
ready to spring upon him, the bull appeared about to gore
him through, the serpent writhed without quite reaching
him, the wolf was rushing straight at him; and the noises
emitted simultaneously by all the apparitions were frightful and the fury shown was fierce.

Antony, pummelled and goaded by them, felt even
severer pain in his body; yet he lay there fearless and all
the more alert in spirit. He groaned, it is true, because of
the pain that racked his body, but his mind was master
of the situation, and as if to mock them, he said: "If you
had any power in you, it would have been enough for just
one of you to come; but the Lord has taken your strength
away, and so you are trying, if possible, to scare me out of
my wits by your numbers. It is a sign of your helplessness
that you ape the forms of brutes." Again he made bold to
say: "If you can, and have received power against me, do
not delay, but up and at me! If you cannot, why excite
yourselves to no purpose? For faith in our Lord is a seal
to us and a wall of safety." So, after trying many ruses,
they gnashed their teeth against him, because they were
only fooling themselves and not him.

10. And here again the Lord was not forgetful of
Antony's struggle, but came to help him. For he looked
up and saw as it were the roof opening and a beam of light

coming down to him. The demons suddenly were gone
and the pain in his body ceased at once and the building
was restored to its former condition. Antony, perceiving
that help had come, breathed more freely and felt relieved
of his pains. And he asked the vision: "Where were you?
Why did you not appear at the beginning to stop my
pains?"

And a voice came to him: "Antony, I was right here,
but I waited to see you in action. And now, because you
held out and did not surrender,[49] I will ever be your helper
and I will make you renowned everywhere." [50]

Hearing this, he arose and prayed; and he was so
strengthened that he felt his body more vigorous than before. He was at this time about thirty-five years old.

HE CROSSES THE NILE. LIFE IN THE DESERT SOLITUDE OF PISPIR

11. On the next day he went out, inspired with an even
greater zeal for the service of God. He met the old man
referred to above and begged him to live with him in the
desert. The other declined because of his age and because
such a mode of life was not yet the custom. So he at once
set out for the mountain by himself. But there was the
Enemy again! Seeing his earnestness and wishing to
thwart it, he projected the illusion of a large disc of silver
into the road. But Antony, seeing through the trickery
of the Hater of Goodness, stopped, and, looking at the
disc, exposed the Devil in it, saying: "A disc in the desert?
Where does that come from? This is not a travelled high-
way, and there is no track of any people coming this way.

It is of great size, it could not have been dropped un-
noticed. Indeed, even if it had been lost, the loser would
have turned back and looked for it; and he would have
found it because this is desert country. This is a trick of
the Devil. You will not thwart my resolution by this,
Devil. Let this thing perish with you." [51] As Antony
said this, it disappeared like smoke leaving fire.

12. Then as he went on, he again saw, not another
illusion, but real gold scattered along the roadside. Now,
whether it was the Enemy that called his attention to it,
or whether it was a good power training the champion
and showing the Devil that he did not care for even
genuine riches, he himself did not indicate, and we do not
know either, except to say that it was gold that appeared
there. As for Antony, he was surprised at the amount of
it, but he stepped over it as though it were fire and passed
on without turning back. Indeed, he started to run so
fast, that presently he lost sight of the place and it lay
hidden from him.

So, having grown stronger and stronger in his purpose,
he hurried to the mountain.[52] On the far side of the river
he found a deserted fort which in the course of time had
become infested with creeping things. There he settled
down to live. The reptiles, as though someone were
chasing them, left at once. He blocked up the entrance,
having laid in bread for six months—this the Thebans do
and often loaves keep fresh for a whole year—and with
water in the place, he disappeared as in a shrine. He
remained there alone, never going forth and never seeing
anyone pass by. For a long time he persisted in this practice of asceticism; only twice a year he received bread
from the house above.

13. His acquaintances who came to see him often spent days and nights outside, since he would not let them come in. They heard what sounded like riotous crowds inside making noises, raising a tumult, wailing piteously and shrieking: "Get out of our domain! What business have you in the desert? You cannot hold out against our persecution." At first those outside thought there were men fighting with him and that they had entered in by means of ladders, but as they peered through a hole and saw no one, they realized that demons were involved; and filled with fear, they called out to Antony. But he was more concerned over hearing them than to pay any attention to the demons. Going close to the door he suggested to them to leave and to have no fear. "It is only against the timid," he said, "that the demons conjure up spectres. You, now, sign yourselves and go home unafraid, and leave them to make fools of themselves." [53]

So they departed, fortified by the Sign of the Cross, while he remained without suffering any harm whatsoever from them. Nor did he grow weary of the contest, for the assistance given him through visions coming to him from on high, and the weakness of his enemies brought him great relief in his hardships and gave him the stamina for greater zeal. His friends would come again and again, expecting, of course, to find him dead; but they heard him singing: *Let God arise and let his enemies be scattered; and let them that hate Him flee from before His face. As smoke vanisheth, so let them vanish away; as wax melteth before the fire, so let the sinners perish before the face of God.*[54] And again: *All nations compassed me about; and in the name of the Lord I drove them off.*[55]

HE LEAVES HIS SOLITUDE. THE FATHER
AND TEACHER OF MONKS

14. So he spent nearly twenty years practicing the ascetic life by himself, never going out and but seldom seen by others. After this, as there were many who longed and sought to imitate his holy life and some of his friends came and forcefully broke down the door and removed it, Antony came forth as out of a shrine, as one initiated into sacred mysteries and filled with the spirit of God. It was the first time that he showed himself outside the fort to those who came to him. When they saw him, they were astonished to see that his body had kept its former appearance, that it was neither obese from want of exercise, nor emaciated from his fastings and struggles with the demons: he was the same man they had known before his retirement.

Again, the state of his soul was pure, for it was neither contracted by grief, nor dissipated by pleasure nor pervaded by jollity or dejection. He was not embarrassed when he saw the crowd, nor was he elated at seeing so many there to receive him. No, he had himself completely under control—a man guided by reason and stable in his character.

Through him the Lord cured many of those present who were afflicted with bodily ills, and freed others from impure spirits. He also gave Antony charm in speaking; and so he comforted many in sorrow, and others who were quarrelling he made friends. He exhorted all to prefer

nothing in the world to the love of Christ. And when in
his discourse he exhorted them to be mindful of the good
things to come and of the goodness shown us by God,
*who spared not His own Son, but delivered Him up for
us all,*[56] he induced many to take up the monastic life.
And so now monasteries [57] also sprang up in the mountains and the desert was populated with monks who left
their own people and registered themselves for citizenship
in Heaven.[58]

15. When the need arose for him to cross the canal of
Arsinoë [59]—and the occasion was a visitation of the brethren—the canal was full of crocodiles. And simply praying,
he went in with all his companions, and passed over unscathed. Returning to his monastery, he zealously applied
himself to his holy and vigorous exercises. By ceaseless
conferences he fired the zeal of those who were already
monks, and incited most of the others to a love of the
ascetic life; and soon, as his message drew men after him,
the number of monasteries multiplied and to all he was a
father and guide.

ANTONY'S ADDRESS TO THE MONKS (16-43)

16. Now, one day when he had gone out, all the monks
came to him and asked to hear a discourse. He spoke to
them in the Egyptian [60] tongue as follows:

"The Scriptures are really sufficient for our instruc-
tion.[61] Yet it is well for us to encourage each other in the
faith and to employ words to stimulate ourselves. Be you,
therefore, like children and bring to your father what you

know and tell it, while I, being your senior, share with you my knowledge and my experience.

"To begin with, let us all have the same zeal, not to give up what we have begun, not to lose heart, nor to say: 'We have spent a long time in this asceticism.' No, beginning over each day, let us increase our zeal. The whole of man's life is very short measured by the ages to come, so that all our time is as nothing compared to eternal life. And in the world everything is sold at its worth and like value is bartered for like; but the promise of eternal life is bought for very little. For Scripture says: *The days of our life have seventy years in them; but if in the mighty they are eighty years and more, they are a labor and a burden.*[62] If, then, we live the full eighty years, or even a hundred, in the practice of asceticism, we shall not reign the same period of a hundred years, but instead of the hundred we shall reign for ever and ever. And though our striving is on earth, we shall not receive our inheritance on earth, but what is promised us is in Heaven. Moreover, we shall put aside our corruptible body, and receive it back incorruptible.[63]

17. "So, children, let us not grow weary nor think that we are toiling a long time or that we are doing something great. For *the sufferings of this present time are not worthy to be compared with the glory to come that shall be revealed to us.*[64] Neither let us look back upon the world and think that we have renounced great things. For even the whole world is a very trifling thing compared with all of Heaven. Accordingly, if we should be lords of the whole earth and renounced the whole earth, this would again mean nothing as compared with the King-

dom of Heaven.[65] As though a person should despise one
copper drachma to gain a hundred drachmas of gold, so
he who is lord of all the earth, and renounces it, really
gives up but little and receives a hundredfold. If, then,
even the whole earth is not equal in value to Heaven, certainly one who gives up a few acres must not boast nor
be careless; for what he leaves behind is practically
nothing, even though it be a home or a tidy sum of
money he parts with.

"We must further bear in mind that if we do not give
up these things for virtue's sake, later we must leave them
behind and often, too, as Ecclesiastes reminds us,[66] even
to persons to whom we do not wish to leave them. Then
why not give them up for virtue's sake so that we may
inherit a kingdom besides? Therefore, let none of us have
even the desire to possess riches. For what does it avail
us to possess what we cannot take with us?[67] Why not
rather possess those things which we can take along
with us—prudence, justice, temperance, fortitude, understanding, charity, love of the poor, faith in Christ, meekness, hospitality? Once we possess these we shall find
them going before us, preparing a welcome for us in the
land of the meek.

18. "With these thoughts let a man persuade himself
that he must not grow careless, and that all the more
as he considers that he is a servant of the Lord and bound
to serve his Master. Now, a servant would not dare to
say, 'Since I worked yesterday, I am not working today.'
Nor will he count up the time that has elapsed and rest
during the days that lie ahead of him; no, day in and
day out, as is written in the Gospel,[68] he shows the same

willingness in order that he may please his master and not incur any trouble. So let us also persist in the daily practice of asceticism, knowing that if we are negligent a single day, He will not forgive us for old time's sake, but will be angry at us because of our carelessness. So, too, we have heard in Ezechiel; [69] so also Judas because of one single night destroyed the toil of an entire past.

19. "Therefore, children, let us persevere in the practice of asceticism and not be careless. For in this also we have the Lord with us to help us, as Scripture says: *God co-operates unto good* [70] with everyone who chooses the good. And that we may not be careless, it is well to think over what the Apostle says, namely, *I die daily*.[71] Indeed, if we, too, live as if we were to die each new day, we shall not sin. As to the quotation given, its meaning is this: when we awaken each day, we should think that we shall not live till evening; and again, when about to go to sleep we should think that we shall not awaken. Our life is by nature uncertain and is measured out to us daily by Providence. If we are so disposed and live our daily life accordingly, we shall not commit sin, nor lust after anything, nor bear a grudge against anyone, nor lay up treasures on earth; but as men who each day expect to die, we shall be poor and we shall forgive everything to all men. As to lusting after women or other sordid pleasure, we shall not entertain such at all, but turn our backs upon it as something transitory—ever fighting on and looking forward to the Day of Judgment. For the fear of greater things involved and the anxiety over torments invariably dissipate the fascination of pleasure and steady the wavering spirit.

20.   "Now that we have made a beginning and set
out on the path of virtue, let us lengthen our steps even
more to reach what lies ahead of us.[72] And let no one
turn back as did Lot's wife,[73] especially since the Lord
has said: *No man putting his hand to the plough and
turning back is fit for the Kingdom of Heaven.*[74] And this
turning back is nothing else than to feel regret and to
set one's mind again on worldly things.

"When you hear virtue mentioned, do not be afraid
of it nor treat it as a foreign word. Really, it is not far
from us, nor is its home apart from us; no, the thing is
within us, and its accomplishment is easy if we but have
the will. Greeks go abroad and cross the sea to study
letters; but we have no need to go abroad for the Kingdom
of Heaven nor to cross the sea to obtain virtue. The Lord
has told us in advance: *The Kingdom of Heaven is
within you.*[75] Virtue, therefore, has need only of our
will, since it is within us and springs from us. Virtue
exists when the soul keeps in its natural state. It is kept
in its natural state when it remains as it came into being.
Now it came into being fair and perfectly straight. Wherefore, Jesus, the son of Nun, exhorted the people in these
words: *Make straight your hearts unto the Lord God
of Israel;*[76] and John: *Make straight your paths.*[77] For
the soul is said to be straight when its mind is in its
natural state as it was created. But when it swerves and
is perverted from its natural condition, that is called
vice of the soul.

"So the task is not difficult: If we remain as we were
made, we are in the state of virtue; but if we give our
minds to base things, we are accounted evil. If the task
had to be accomplished from without, it would indeed

be difficult; but since this is within us, let us guard ourselves from foul thoughts. And having received the soul
as something entrusted to us, let us guard it for the Lord,
that He may recognize His work as being the same as
He made it.

21. "Let us also struggle for this, that anger be not
our master, nor concupiscence enslave us. For it is written that *the anger of man worketh not the justice of God.*[78]
And concupiscence, *when it hath conceived, bringeth
forth sin; and sin, when it is completed, begetteth death.*[79]
Living this life, let us be carefully on our guard and, as
is written, *with all watchfulness keep our heart.*[80] For we
have enemies, powerful and crafty—the wicked demons;
and it is against these that *our wrestling is,* as the Apostle
said—*not against flesh and blood, but against principalities
and powers, against the rulers of the world of this darkness, against the spirits of wickedness in the high places.*[81]
Great is the number of them in the air around us,[82] and
they are not far from us. But the difference between them
is considerable. It would take us too long to give an
account of their nature and distinctions, and such a
disquisition is for others greater than we: [83] the one urgent
and necessary thing for us now is merely to know their
villainies against us.

22. "Now, first of all, let us realize this: that the
demons were not made demons as we understand the
term, for God made nothing bad. They, too, were created fair, but they fell away from heavenly wisdom. Since
then they have been roaming the earth. On the one
hand, they have deceived the Greeks[84] with vain fancies;[85]
and, envious of us Christians, they leave nothing undone

to hinder us from entering Heaven: they do not want us
to mount to the place from which they have fallen. Hence,
too, the necessity of much prayer and ascetic discipline
that one may receive through the Holy Spirit the gift of
discerning spirits and may be able to know about them [86]—
which of them are less wicked, which of them are more
so; and what special interest each one of them pursues
and how each is rebuffed and cast out. For their ruses
and machinations are numerous. Of this the blessed
Apostle and his followers were aware when they said:
For we are not ignorant of his devices.[87] And we, draw-
ing on our experiences with them, ought to guide each
other aright, away from them. Hence I, having made
this experience in part, speak to you as to my children.

23. "If, then, they see Christians in general, but monks
in particular, working cheerfully and making progress,
they first assail them and tempt them by continually placing stumbling blocks in their way.[88] These stumbling
blocks are evil thoughts. But we must not be afraid of
their waylayings, for by prayers and fastings and confidence in the Lord they are promptly thwarted. Yet,
though thwarted, they do not cease, but return to the
attack with all wickedness and cunning.[89] When they
cannot deceive the heart by manifestly unclean pleasure,
they change their tactics and march to the attack again.
They then devise and affect apparitions in order to
frighten it, transforming themselves and mimicking
women, beasts, reptiles, and bodies of huge size and
hordes of warriors. But even so we must not cower at
these their phantoms, for they are nothing and quickly
vanish, especially if a person fortifies himself with the
Sign of the Cross.[90]

"Indeed, they are daring and exceedingly shameless. If here, too, they suffer defeat, they advance once more with new strategy. They pretend to prophesy and to foretell future events. They show themselves taller than the roof and burly and bulky. Their purpose is, if possible, to snatch off by such phantoms those whom they could not deceive with thoughts. And should they find that even so the soul remains fortified by its faith and the hope it entertains, then they bring in their chief."

24. "And often," he said, "they appear in such fashion; as, for instance, the Lord revealed the Devil to Job saying: *His eyes are as the appearance of dawn. From his mouth come forth burning lamps, and fires are shot forth. From his nostrils comes the smoke of a furnace burning with a fire of coals. His breath is coals, and flame proceeds from his mouth.*[91] When the chief of the demons appears in this way, the knave tries to terrorize us, as I said before, by his braggart talk, and that again as he was unmasked by the Lord saying to Job: *He esteemed iron as chaff, and bronze as rotten wood; he deemed the sea a vessel of ointment and the depth of the abyss as a captive; he judged the abyss to be a place for walking;*[92] and through the Prophet: *The enemy said: 'I will pursue and overtake';*[93] and through another: *I will grasp the whole world in my hand like a nest, and as abandoned eggs will I take it up.*[94]

"Such, in short, are the boastings they resort to and such the declamations they make in order to deceive the God-fearing. Here, again, we faithful need not fear his appearances nor pay attention to his words. He is only a liar and there is no truth in all that he speaks. When he talks such stuff and does this with so much boasting, he overlooks how he was dragged with a hook like a dragon by the Savior, haltered around his snout like a beast of burden, and had his nostrils ringed like a runaway and his lips pierced through by an iron band. He has also been bound by the Lord as a sparrow for our amusement.[95] Both he and his fellow demons have been made so as to be trodden under foot like scorpions and snakes [96] by us Christians; and proof of this is the fact that we are now existing in spite of him. Indeed, note that he who proclaimed that he would dry up the sea and seize the whole world, cannot hinder our ascetic practices nor even stop me speaking against him. Wherefore, let us not pay attention to what he may say—he is a plain liar—nor fear his apparitions, for they are lies too. Indeed, it is not true light which appears in them, rather they are a mere beginning and semblance of the fire prepared for them; and it is with that in which they will be burned that they try to terrify mankind. They do appear, it is true, but disappear again the same moment, without harming any of the faithful, while taking with them a likeness of the fire that is to receive them. So here there is no reason either for fearing them; for by the grace of Christ all their tactics come to naught.

25. "But they are treacherous and prepared to undergo every change and transformation. Often, for instance, they even pretend to sing Psalms without appearing, and to quote sayings from Scripture. Sometimes, too, when we are reading they at once repeat like an echo what we have read. When we go to bed they rouse us to prayers; and this they carry on continuously, scarcely permitting

us to sleep at all. At other times again they put on the guise of monks and simulate pious talk, having in mind to practice deception by their assumed likeness and then to drag off the victims where they will. But we must not pay attention to them, even if they rouse us to prayer, even if they advise us not to eat at all, even if they pretend to accuse and revile us for what they once approved. It is not for the sake of piety or for truth's sake that they do this, but in order to bring the guileless into despair; and to represent the ascetical life as worthless, and to make men disgusted with the solitary life as something coarse and all too burdensome, and to trip up those who live such a life in spite of them.

26. "Hence the Prophet sent by the Lord called such as these unhappy in these terms: *Woe to him that giveth his neighbor a troubled drink.*[97] For such tactics and arguments are ruinous of the way that leads to virtue. Our Lord Himself, even though the demons spoke the truth— for they said truly; *Thou art the Son of God* [98]—nevertheless silenced them and forbade them to speak. He did not want them to sow their own evil along with truth; and He also had in mind to accustom us never to heed them even though they should appear to speak the truth. Then, too, it is unbecoming that we who possess the Sacred Scriptures and the freedom of the Savior, should be taught by the Devil, by him who has not remained at his post,[99] but has changed his mind constantly. Hence, He also forbids him to use quotations from the Scriptures, saying: *But to the sinner God hath said: 'Why do you relate my judgments and take my testament into your mouth?'* [100] Indeed, they do everything: they talk, they raise clamor,

they practice deception, they cause confusion—all to beguile the simple. They also din loudly, emit silly laughs,
and hiss. If no one pays any attention to them, they wail
and lament as though defeated.

27.   "The Lord, therefore, because He is God, silenced
the demons. As for us, we have learned our lessons from
the Saints and do as they have done and imitate their
courage. For when they saw such things, they made it
their practice to say: *When the sinner stood against me,
I was dumb, and was humbled, and kept silence from good
things;* [101] and again: *But I, as a deaf man, heard not; and
as a dumb man not opening his mouth; and I became as a
man that heareth not.* [102] So let us, too, neither listen to
them, regarding them as so many strangers, nor pay any
attention to them, though they rouse us to prayer and
talk about fasting. Let us rather attend to the practice of
asceticism as resolved upon by us and not be misled by
them who practice treachery in all they do. We must not
fear them even though they appear to attack us and to
threaten death. In reality, they are weak and can do
nothing but threaten.

28.   "Well, up to this point I have spoken on this subject only in passing. But now I must not shrink from
dealing with it in greater detail: to bring this to your
attention can only redound to your greater safety.

"Since the Lord dwelt with us, the Enemy is fallen and
his powers have declined. [103] Therefore, he can do nothing; still, though he is fallen, like a tyrant he does not
keep quiet, but threatens even if his threats are but words.
And let each one of you bear this in mind, and he can
despise the demons. Now, if they were bound to such

bodies as we are, they might then say: 'People who hide themselves we do not find; but if we do find them, we do them harm.' And in that case we could escape them by hiding and locking the doors against them. But since this is not the case and they can enter despite locked doors; and seeing that they are present everywhere in the air, they and their leader, the Devil; and if they are evil-willed and bent on doing harm and if, as the Savior said, *the father of evil, the Devil, is a murderer from the beginning:* [104] then, if nevertheless we live and live our lives in defiance of him, it is plain that they are without any power. For, as you see, place does not hinder their plotting, neither do they see us friendly to them, that they should spare us, nor are they lovers of good, that they should change their ways. No, on the contrary, they are wicked, and there is nothing they desire more eagerly than to harm lovers of virtue and worshippers of God. For the simple reason that they are impotent to do anything, they do nothing except threaten. If they could, you may be sure that they would not wait, but effect what is uppermost in their desires—evil, and that especially against us. Note, for instance, how we are gathered here and speaking against them, and that they know that as we make progress they grow weak. Indeed, if it were within their power, they would not let one of us Christians live, for the service of God is an abomination to the sinner. [105] And since they can do nothing, it is rather themselves they hurt, for they cannot carry out any of their threats.

"Further, this should also be taken into account to put an end to fear of them: if they had any power, they would not come in droves, nor resort to apparitions, nor would

they employ the device of transforming themselves. But
it would be enough that one only should come and do
what he is able and inclined to do; and, most important
of all, anyone who really has power neither endeavors to
slay with phantoms nor seeks to terrify with hordes, but
without further ado uses his power as he wills. But actually the demons, powerless as they are, cut capers as if
they were on a stage, changing their forms and frightening children by the illusion of coming in hordes and by
the grimaces they make—all things for which they are
the more to be despised as weaklings. To be sure, the
genuine angel sent by the Lord against the Assyrians had
no need of crowds, nor of visible illusions, nor of resound-
ing blows or rattling noises; no, he exercised his power
quietly and straightway put to death one hundred and
eighty-five thousand of them.[106] But the demons, impotent creatures that they are, try to terrify, and if it be by
mere phantoms!

29. "Now, if any one should ponder the story of Job
and say: 'Why, then, did the Devil go forth and do everything against him? He stripped him of his possessions,
killed his children, and struck him with a grievous ulcer,[107]
—let such a person realize that this was not a case of the
Devil having the power to do this, but of God turning
over Job to him to be tried.[108] Of course, he had no power
to do it; he asked for it and did this when he received it.
So, here again there is the more reason to despise the
Enemy, for although such was his desire, he could not
prevail against even one just man. Had the power been
his, he evidently would not have asked for it; and the
fact that he asked not once, but a second time, exposes
his weakness and inability. Nor is it extraordinary that

he had no power against Job, when it was impossible for him to destroy even his herds unless God had acceded to it. No, not even against swine does he have power, as is written in the Gospel: *They besought the Lord, saying: 'Let us depart into the swine.'* [109] But if they have no power even over swine, much less do they have power over men made after the image of God.[110]

30. "Wherefore, one must fear God alone and despise those beings and not fear them at all. But the more they do these things, the more let us devote ourselves to asceticism to counteract them, for an upright life and faith in God is a great weapon against them. Indeed, they dread ascetics for their fasting, their vigils, their prayers; their meekness, calmness, contempt of money, lack of conceit, humility, love of the poor, almsgiving, freedom from anger, and, most of all, their loyalty to Christ. This is the reason they do everything that no one may trample them under foot. They know the grace given to the faithful by the Savior when He said: *Behold, I have given you power to trample upon serpents and scorpions and upon all the power of the enemy.* [111]

31. "Again, if they pretend also to foretell the future, let no one give heed. Often, for instance, they tell us days beforehand of brothers coming to visit us; and they do come. But it is not because they care for their hearers that they do this, but in order to induce them to place their confidence in them, and then, when they have them well in hand, to destroy them. Hence, we must not listen to them, but send them off, for we have no need of them. What is wonderful about that, if they who have lighter bodies than men,[112] seeing that men have set out on a

journey, outdistance them and announce their arrival? A person riding horseback could outstrip a man journeying on foot and give the same advance information. So, once again there is no need to marvel at them. They have no fore-knowledge of what has not yet happened,[113] but God alone knows all things before they come into being.[114] These, however, are like thieves in that they run ahead and announce what they see. At this very moment to how many have they made known our business, how we have gathered here and hold a discussion against them, before anyone of us can leave and report the same! But a boy fast on his feet could do the same, getting ahead of a slower person.

"What I am trying to say is this. If someone were to take to the road from the Thebaid or any other place, until he actually starts, they do not know whether he will go on a journey; but once they see him walking, they run ahead and announce him before his arrival. And it so happens that after a few days he arrives. Often, though, travellers turn back and their report is false.

32. "So, too, they sometimes talk nonsense in regard to the water of the River.[115] For example, seeing heavy rains falling in the regions of Ethiopia and knowing that the flooding of the River originates there, they run ahead and tell it before the water reaches Egypt. Men could tell it too, if they could run as fast as these.[116] And as David's lookout-man,[117] mounting a height, got an earlier glimpse of who was coming than did the one who was staying below;[118] and as the man who ran ahead brought tidings before the rest, not of what had not yet come to pass, but of things already on the way to be reported and actually happening, so these choose to hasten and announce things

to others for the sole reason of deceiving them. Indeed, if in the meantime Providence were to make a special disposition in regard to the waters or the travellers—and this is quite possible—then the demons' report turns out to be a lie and those who put trust in them are deceived.

33. "Thus it was that the Greek oracles arose and thus the people of old were led astray by the demons.[119] But with this also goes the story of how deception was stopped for the future. For the Lord came who suppressed the demons along with their villainy. For they know nothing of themselves, but they see what knowledge others have, and like thieves they pick it up and misrepresent it. They practice guesswork rather than prophecy. Wherefore, even if they should sometimes hit on the truth in speaking of such things, even so a person must not wonder at them. Indeed, physicians, too, who are experts in diseases from having observed the same ailment in different persons, often make conjectures on the basis of their practice and foretell what will happen. And again, pilots and farmers, observing the weather conditions, forecast from their experience if there will be a storm or fair weather. But no one would say because of this that they prophesy by divine inspiration, but by experience and practice. Consequently, if the demons, too, sometimes guess at these same things and mention them, you must not therefore be astonished at them nor mind them at all. Of what use is it to the hearers to know from them days in advance what is going to happen? Or what point is there to eagerness to know such things, even if such knowledge prove true? Surely, this is not the stuff of which virtue is made, nor is it at all a token of good character. For no one of us is judged by

what he does not know, and no one is called blessed because of what he has learned and knows; no, the judgment that awaits each asks this—whether he has kept the faith and faithfully observed the commandments.

34. "Hence, it behooves us not to make much of these things, nor to give ourselves to the toil of asceticism for the sake of knowing the future, but that we may please God by living well. And we should pray, not in order to know the future, nor should we ask for this as a reward for the practice of asceticism, but that the Lord may be our fellow worker in achieving victory over the Devil. But if we care some day to know the future, let us be pure in mind. For I feel confident that if the soul is pure through and through and is in its natural state,[120] it becomes clear-sighted and sees more and farther than the demons.[121] It then has the Lord to reveal things to it. Such was the soul of Eliseus seeing what went on with Giezi,[122] and beholding the armies standing nearby.[123]

35. "Now then, when they come to you at night and want to tell the future, or say, 'We are the angels,' ignore them, for they are lying. If they praise your practice of asceticism and call you blessed, do not listen to them nor have anything to do with them at all. Rather sign yourselves and your dwelling and pray; and you will see them disappear. They simply are cowards and deathly afraid of the Sign of our Lord's Cross, since it was on the Cross that the Savior stripped them and made an example of them.[124] But if they persist even more shamelessly, dancing about and changing their appearance, do not fear them, nor cower, nor give them any attention as though they were good; for it is quite possible to tell the difference

between the good and the bad when God grants it.[125] A vision of the holy ones is not turbulent, for *he shall not contend, nor cry out, neither shall any man hear his voice.*[126] But it comes so quietly and gently that instantly joy and gladness and courage arise in the soul. For with them is our Lord who is our joy, and the power of God the Father. And the thoughts of the soul remain untroubled and unruffled,[127] so that in its own bright transparency it is able to behold those who appear. A longing for things divine and for the things of the future life takes possession of it, and its desire is that it may be wholly united to them if it could but depart with them. But if some, being human, are seized with fear at the vision of the good, then those who appear dispel the fear by love, as did Gabriel for Zachary,[128] and the angel who appeared to the women at the holy sepulchre,[129] and the angel who spoke to the shepherds in the Gospel: *Fear not.*[130] Fear in these cases is not from cravenness of soul, but from an awareness of the presence of higher beings. Such, then, is the vision of the holy ones.

36. "On the other hand, the attack and appearance of the evil ones is full of confusion, accompanied by crashing, roaring, and shouting: it could well be the tumult produced by rude boys and robbers. This at once begets terror in the soul, disturbance and confusion of thoughts, dejection, hatred of ascetics, indifference, sadness, remembrance of kinsfolk, and fear of death; and then a desire for evil, a disdain for virtue, and a complete subversion of character. When, therefore, you have a vision and are afraid, if then the fear is taken from you immediately and in its place comes ineffable joy and contentment; and

courage and recovery of strength and calmness of thought and the other things I have mentioned, and stoutheartedness, too, and love of God, then be of good cheer and pray—for your joy and your soul's tranquillity betoken the holiness of Him who is present. Thus Abraham, seeing the Lord, rejoiced; [131] and John, hearing the voice of Mary, the Mother of God,[132] leaped for joy.[133] But when you have certain visions, and confusion overtakes you and there is tumult from without and earthly apparitions and threats of death and all the things I have mentioned, then know that the visit is from the wicked.

37. "And let this also be a sign to you: when the soul remains in fear, it is enemies that are present. For the demons do not take away fear caused by them as did the great archangel Gabriel for Mary and Zachary and he who appeared to the women at the sepulchre; [134] on the contrary, when they see men afraid, they increase their phantoms that they may terrify them the more, and then descend upon them and mock them, saying: *Fall down and adore us.*[135] In this way they deceived the Greeks, for among them they were thus taken falsely for gods. But our Lord did not permit us to be deceived by the Devil, when once He rebuked him for trying to pass off such phantoms on Him: *Get behind me, Satan; for it is written, 'The Lord thy God shalt thou adore and Him only shalt thou serve.'* [136] Therefore, let the Author of Evil be more and more despised by us, for what our Lord has said, that He has done for our sake: that when the demons hear like words from us, they may be driven off through the Lord who in those words rebuked them.

38. "We must not boast about casting out demons, nor

give ourselves airs because of cures performed; nor must we honor only him who casts out demons and hold in contempt one who does not. Let a man study closely the ascetic life of each, and then either imitate and emulate it, or else correct it. For to work miracles [137] is not for us. That is reserved for the Savior. Indeed, He said to the disciples: *Rejoice not because demons are subject to you, but because your names are written in Heaven.*[138] And the fact that our names are inscribed in Heaven is witness to our life of virtue, but as to casting out demons, that is the gift of the Savior who grants it. Hence, to those who were boasting not of their virtue, but of their miracles, and saying: *Lord, have we not cast out devils in Thy name and wrought many miracles in Thy name?*[139] He answered: *Amen, I say to you, I know you not;*[140] for the Lord knows not the ways of the ungodly.[141] In short, one must pray, as I have said, for the gift of discerning spirits, that, as is written, we may not put faith in every spirit.[142]

39. "Really, I meant to stop and to mention nothing coming from my own self, satisfied with what has been said. That you may not think, however, that I simply say these things, but may be convinced that I am speaking from experience and truth, for this reason I here recount what I have seen of the practices of the demons. I shall perhaps appear foolish; even so the Lord who listens knows that my conscience is clear and that it is not for myself, but out of my love for you and to encourage you that I do so.

"How often they called me blessed, while I cursed them in the name of the Lord! How often they made predictions regarding the water of the River and I said to them,

'And what business is that of yours?' Once they came
with threats and surrounded me like soldiers in full armor.
On another occasion they filled the house with horses and
beasts and reptiles, but I chanted the Psalm: *These are
in chariots and these are on horses, but we shall be mag-
nified in the name of the Lord God,*[143] and at these prayers
they were repulsed by the Lord. Once in the dark they
came with an illusion of light and said: 'We have come
to bring you light, Antony.' But I shut my eyes, I prayed,
and at once the light of the impious ones was put out.
And a few months later they came along chanting Psalms
and quoting the Scriptures. But *I as one deaf heard not.*[144]
Once they shook the monastery [145] from one side to the
other, but I prayed, remaining unshaken in mind. Then
they came again and made a continuous noise, hammer-
ing, hissing, and prancing about. But I prayed and lay
singing Psalms to myself; and presently they began to
wail and cry, as though completely exhausted; and I ex-
tolled the Lord who had brought to naught their brazen-
ness and madness and taught them a lesson.

40. "Once a very tall demon appeared in a vision and
dared to say: 'I am the power of God'; and, 'I am Providence. What favor do you wish me to bestow upon you?'
Then I blew a breath at him,[146] calling upon the name of
Christ, and I made an effort to strike him. It would seem
that I succeeded, and instantly, big as he was, he with all
his fellow demons disappeared at the name of Christ.
Once when I was fasting, the Crafty One came to me
even as a monk carrying phantom loaves. He counselled
me, saying: 'Eat, and cease from your many hardships!
You, too, are a man and you are bound to get sick.' But I,
perceiving his wiliness, arose to pray, and he could not

bear it. He left, resembling smoke as he went out through the door.

"How often in the desert did he show me a vision of gold that I might but touch it and look at it! But I would counter him by chanting a Psalm and it would be dissolved. Often they struck me blows, and I would say: 'Nothing will separate me from the love of Christ'; [147] and then they would beat each other instead! But it was not I who stopped them and crippled their efforts, but it was the Lord, He who says: *I saw Satan like lightning falling from Heaven.*[148]

"My children, mindful of what the Apostle said, *I have applied this to myself*,[149] that you may learn not to lose heart in your ascetic life, and not to fear the delusions of the Devil and his demons.

41. "And, seeing that I have already made myself foolish by going into all this, take the following, too, to serve your own safety and self-assurance; and believe me— I am not lying.

"Once there was a knock at my door in the monastery, and going out I saw a tall, towering figure. Then, when I asked, 'Who are you?'

'I am Satan,' he said.

'What are you doing here?' I asked him.

He said: 'Why do the monks and all the other Christians find fault with me for no reason at all? Why do they curse me every hour?'

'Well,' said I, 'why do you annoy them?'

He said: 'It is not I who annoy them, but their troubles originate with themselves; for I have become weak. Have they not read: *The swords of the enemy have failed to the end and their cities Thou hast destroyed?*[150] I now have

no place, no weapon, no city. Everywhere there are
Christians, and even the desert is already full of monks.[151]
Let them mind their own business and not curse me with-
out cause.'

"Then I marvelled at the grace of the Lord and said to
him: 'Though you are always the liar and never speak
the truth, yet this time you have spoken the truth, however you disliked to do so. You see, Christ by His coming
had made you powerless and cast you down and stripped
you.' He, hearing the Savior's name and unable to endure
the heat it caused in him, vanished.

42. "Wherefore, if even the Devil himself confesses
that he has no power, we ought to condemn him and his
demons as well from first to last. The Evil One with his
hounds, it is true, has all this store of knaveries; but we,
having learned their weakness, can despise them. Let us,
therefore, not give up and become despondent in mind,
nor entertain cowardice in our soul, nor conjure up fears
for ourselves, saying—'If only a demon does not come and
trip me up! If only he does not lift me up and hurl me
down, or appear suddenly and scare me out of my wits!'
No, we must not have such thoughts at all nor grieve as
though we were perishing. Let us rather be of good
courage and rejoice always as men who are being saved.
Let us ponder in our soul that the Lord is with us, He
who put the evil spirits to flight and made them impotent.

"Let us think this over and ever bear in mind that as
long as the Lord is with us, our enemies will do us no
harm. For when they come, they conduct themselves as
they find us; and in whatever state of mind they find us,
so likewise do they represent their phantoms.[152] If they

see us panic-stricken with fear, they promptly take possession like robbers who find the place unguarded; and whatever we think of ourselves, this they pay out with interest added. If they see us fearful and fainthearted, so much the more do they augment our faithheartedness in the form of phantoms and threats, and thus the poor soul is tormented for the future. But if they find us rejoicing in the Lord, meditating on the good things to come and contemplating the things that are the Lord's, considering that everything is in the Lord's hands and that a demon has no power over a Christian, that, in fact, he has no power over anyone at all—then, seeing the soul safeguarded with thoughts such as these, they are put to shame and they turn away. Thus, when the Enemy saw Job fortified all round, he withdrew from him, but finding Judas bare of all this, he took him prisoner.

"Wherefore, if we wish to despise the Enemy, let us always keep our thoughts upon the things of the Lord and let the soul ever rejoice in hope.[153] We shall then see the trumperies of the demons as so much smoke and see them fleeing rather than pursuing. For they are, as I said, abject cowards, always apprehensive of [154] the fire which has been prepared for them.[155]

43. "And observe this, too, as betokening the fearlessness you should have in their presence. When any phantom appears, do not promptly collapse with cowardly fear, but whatever it may be, first ask with stout heart, 'Who are you and whence do you come?' And if it should be a vision of the good, they will reassure you and change your fear into joy. If, however, it has to do with the Devil, it will weaken on the spot, seeing your steadfast mind; for

to simply ask, 'Who are you and whence do you come?'
is an indication of calmness. Thus did the son of Nave in-
quire and learn; [156] and the Enemy did not escape detection when Daniel questioned him." [157]

MONASTIC VIRTUE

44. As Antony discussed these matters with them, all
rejoiced. In some the love of virtue increased, in some
negligence was discarded, and in others conceit was
checked. All heeded his advice to despise the schemings
of the Devil, and were in admiration of the grace given to
Antony by the Lord for the discerning of spirits.

So, then, their solitary cells in the hills were like tents
filled with divine choirs—singing Psalms, studying, fasting, praying, rejoicing in the hope of the life to come, and
laboring in order to give alms and preserving love and
harmony among themselves. And truly it was like seeing
a land apart, a land of piety and justice. For there was
neither wrongdoer nor sufferer of wrong, nor was there
reproof of the tax-collector; [158] but a multitude of ascetics,
all with one set purpose—virtue. Thus, if one saw these
solitary cells again and the fine disposition of the monks,
he could but lift up his voice and say: *How fair are thy
dwellings, O Jacob—thy tents, O Israel! Like shady glens
and like a garden by a river, and like tents that the Lord
hath pitched and cedars beside the waters!* [159]

45. Antony himself went back as usual to his own cell
and intensified his ascetic practices. Day by day he sighed
as he meditated on the heavenly mansions,[160] longing for

them and seeing the short-lived existence of man. When he was about to eat and sleep and provide for the other needs of the body, shame overcame him as he thought of the spiritual nature of the soul.[161] Often when about to partake of food with many other monks, the thought of spiritual food came upon him and he would beg to be excused and went a long way from them, thinking that he should be ashamed to be seen eating by others. He did eat, of course, by himself because his body needed it; and frequently, too, with the brethren—embarrassed because of them, yet speaking freely because of the help his words gave them. He used to say that one should give all one's time to the soul rather than to the body. True, because necessity demands it, a little time should be given to the body; but on the whole we should give our first attention to the soul and look to its advantage. It must not be dragged down by the pleasures of the body, but rather the body must be made subject to the soul. This, he stated, was what the Savior said: *Be not solicitous for your life, what you shall eat, nor for your body what you shall put on. And seek not you what you shall eat or what you shall drink, and be not lifted up on high; for all these things do the nations of the world seek. But your Father knoweth that you have need of all these things. But seek you first His kingdom and all these things shall be added to you.*[162]

THE CANDIDATE FOR MARTYRDOM UNDER
MAXIMIN DAJA (311)

46. After this the persecution of Maximin [163] which broke out at the time befell the Church. When the holy martyrs were taken to Alexandria, he, too, left his cell and followed, saying: "Let us also go to take part in the contest if we are called, or to look on the contestants." Now, he had a yearning to suffer martyrdom, but as he did not wish to give himself up, he ministered to the confessors in the mines and in the prisons.[164] He was busy in the courtroom [165] stimulating the zeal of the contestants as they were called up, and receiving and escorting them as they went to their martyrdom and remaining with them until they had expired. So the judge, seeing his fearlessness and that of his companions and their zeal in this matter, gave orders that no monk was to appear in the court or stay in the city at all. All the others thought it well to remain in hiding that day, but Antony thought so little of it that he washed his clothes [166] and on the following day posted himself at a prominent place in front, in plain view of the prefect. While all wondered at this and the prefect saw it too as he came through with his staff, he stood there unafraid, showing the eager spirit characteristic of us Christians; for, as I stated before, he was praying that he, too, might be martyred. Therefore, he also appeared grieved that he did not suffer martyrdom. [167]

But the Lord was guarding him for our own good and for the good of others, that to many he might be a teacher of the ascetic life which he himself had learned from the

Scriptures. In fact, many from merely seeing his conduct were zealous followers of his way of life. Again, therefore, he followed his wont of ministering to the confessors; and as though he were in bonds with them,[168] he grew weary in his toil for them.

THE DAILY MARTYR OF THE MONASTIC LIFE

47. When the persecution finally ceased and Bishop Peter of blessed memory had suffered martyrdom,[169] he left and went back to his solitary cell; and there he was a daily martyr to his conscience, ever fighting the battles of the Faith. For he practiced a zealous and more intense ascetic life. He fasted continually, his clothing was hair on the inside while the outside was skin,[170] and this he kept to his dying day. He never bathed his body in water to remove filth,[171] nor did he as much as wash his feet or even allow himself to put them in water without necessity. No one ever saw him undressed, nor did anyone ever look upon his bare body till he died and was buried.

48. Now, then, as he returned to solitude and having determined to set himself a period of time during which he would neither go out himself nor receive anyone, a military officer, a certain Martinianus, came to importune Antony: he had a daughter troubled by a demon. As he persisted in staying, knocking at the door, and begging him to come and pray to God for his child, Antony would not open, but using a peephole, he said: "Man, why do you make all this clamor to me? I am a man just as you are. If you believe in Christ whom I serve, go, and, as you

believe, pray to God and it will come to pass." And the man left at once, believing and invoking Christ, and his daughter was cleansed from the demon. Many other things, too, did the Lord perform through him, He who said: *Ask, and it shall be given you.*[172] For very many sufferers simply slept outside his cell,[173] since he would not open his door to them; and they were healed by their faith and sincere prayer.

FLIGHT TO THE INNER MOUNTAIN

49. When he saw himself beset by many and that he was not permitted to withdraw as he had proposed to himself and wished, and concerned that because of what the Lord was doing through him [174] he might become conceited or another might account him more than was proper, he looked about and set out on a journey to the Upper Thebaid to people among whom he was unknown. He had received loaves from the brethren and was sitting by the banks of the River, watching to see if a boat should come along on which he could embark and leave with them. While he was thus on the lookout, a voice came to him from above: "Antony, where are you going, and why?"

He was not bewildered, but, being used to hearing such calls often, he listened and answered: "Since the crowds do not permit me to be alone, therefore I want to go to the Upper Thebaid because of the many annoyances I am subjected to here and especially because they ask me things beyond my power."

"Whether you go up to the Thebaid," the voice said, "or, as you have been considering, down to the Pastures,[175] you will have more—yes, twice as much trouble to put up with. But if you really wish to be by yourself, then go up to the inner desert."

"And," said Antony, "who will show me the way? I am not acquainted with it." At once his attention was called to some Saracens [176] who were about to take that route. Coming up and approaching them, Antony asked to go along with them into the desert. They welcomed him as though by the command of Providence. And he journeyed with them three days and three nights and came to a very high mountain. At the base of the mountain there was water, crystal-clear, sweet, and very cold. Spreading out from there was flat land and a few scraggy date-palms.

50. Antony, as though inspired by God, fell in love with the place,[177] for this was what He meant who spoke to him at the riverbank. He made a beginning by getting some loaves of bread from his companion travellers, and stayed alone on the mountain, with no one to keep him company. For the future he regarded this place as though he had found his own home. As for the Saracens, noticing Antony's enthusiasm, they made it a point to travel through by that road and were happy to bring him bread. Then, too, in those days he derived a small and frugal change of diet from the date-palms. Later the brethren, learning of the place, like children mindful of their father, saw to it that bread was sent to him. Antony, however, seeing that the bread was causing some of them to trouble themselves to the extent of enduring hardship, and mean-

ing to show consideration for the monks in this also, he thought the matter over and asked some of those who visited him to bring him a two-pronged hoe, an axe, and some grain.

When these were brought, he went over the ground about the mountain, and finding a small patch that was suitable, and with a generous supply of water available from the spring, he tilled and sowed it. This he did every year and it furnished him his bread. He was happy that he should not have to trouble anyone for this and that in all things he kept himself from being a burden. But later, seeing that people were coming to him again, he began to raise a few vegetables too, that the visitor might have a little something to restore him after the weariness of that hard road.

At first wild animals in the desert coming for water often would damage the beds in his garden. But he caught one of the animals, held it gently, and said to them all: "Why do you do harm to me when I harm none of you? Go away, and in the Lord's name do not come near these things again!" And ever afterwards, as though awed by his orders, they did not come near the place.[178]

DEMONS AGAIN

51. So he was alone in the Inner Mountain, giving his time to prayer and to the practice of asceticism. But the brethren who looked after him asked that they might come every month and bring him olives and pulse and oil, for he was now an old man.

From those who visited him we have learned how many wrestlings [179] he endured while living there, *not against flesh and blood,* as is written,[180] but in conflict with demons. For there, too, they heard tumults and many voices and clangor as of weapons. At night they saw the mountain alive with wild beasts. They also saw him fighting as with visible foes, and praying against them. To such as visited him he spoke words of encouragement, while for himself he kept up the struggle on bended knees and praying to the Lord. And it was truly remarkable that, alone as he was in such a wilderness, he was neither dismayed by the attacks of the demons, nor, with all the animals and creeping things there, did he fear their savageness. But, as Scripture has it, he truly *trusted in the Lord like Mount Sion,*[181] with a mind unshaken and unruffled. Thus the demons rather fled from him, and the wild beasts, as is written,[182] kept peace with him.

52. So the Devil kept a close watch on Antony and gnashed his teeth against him, as David says in the Psalm; [183] but Antony was heartened by the Savior, remaining unharmed by his villainy and his subtle strategy. Thus, he set wild beasts on him as he kept vigil in the night; and well-nigh all the hyenas in that desert came out of their lairs and encircled him. With him in their midst, each with open jaw threatened to bite him. But he, knowing well the Enemy's craft, said to them all: "If you have received the power to do this against me, I am ready to be devoured by you; if you have been sent by demons, get out without delay, for I am Christ's servant." [184] As Antony was saying this, they fled, as though hounded by the whip of that word.[185]

53. Then a few days later as he was at work—for work was ever in his thoughts—someone came to the door and pulled the cord he was working with: he was weaving baskets, articles he gave to visitors in exchange for what they brought him. He rose and saw a monster resembling a man as far as the thighs, but having legs and feet like an ass. Antony simply made the Sign of the Cross and said: "I am Christ's servant. If you are on a mission against me, here I am." But the monster with its demons fled so fast that its speed caused it to fall and die. And the death of the monster stood for the fall of the demons: they were making every effort to drive him back from the desert, and they could not.

ANTONY VISITS THE BRETHREN ALONG THE NILE

54. Once the monks asked him to return to them and to spend some time on a visitation of them and their settlements. He made the journey with the monks who had come to meet him. A camel carried bread and water for them; for all the desert thereabouts is without water and there is no drinking water at all except in the one mountain from which they had drawn it, there where his cell is. Now, on the way the water gave out and they all were in danger, as the heat was most intense. They went about and returned without finding water. Presently they were too weak to even walk. They stretched themselves out upon the ground and let the camel go, giving themselves up in despair.

Then the old man, seeing the danger all were in, was overcome with grief. Sighing deeply, he walked a little way from them. He then knelt down, stretched forth his hands, and prayed. And at once the Lord made a spring come forth where he was praying, and so all drank and were refreshed.[186] Filling their waterskins, they set out to look for the camel and found it; for it so happened that the rope had wrapped around a stone and it was held fast. They brought it back and watered it, and putting the waterskins on it, finished their journey no worse for the incident.

As he came to the outer cells, all gave him a hearty welcome, regarding him as a father. And he, for his part, as though bringing them provisions from his mountain, entertained them with his stories and gave them of his practical experience. And again there was joy in the mountains and eagerness for improvement, and the consolations that come from a common faith.[187] And so he, too, rejoiced to witness the zeal of the monks and his sister grown old in her virginity, herself the guiding spirit of other virgins.

THE BRETHREN VISIT ANTONY

55. After some days he returned to his mountain. From then on many came to him, and there were those, too, who had an affliction and risked the journey to him. But as for all the monks who came to him, he had the same advice—to place their confidence in the Lord and to love Him, to keep themselves from bad thoughts and pleasures of the flesh, and not to be seduced by a full

stomach, as is written in Proverbs.[188] They should flee conceit and pray continually, sing Psalms before sleeping and after, commit to heart the commandments enjoined in the Scriptures, and hark back to the deeds of the saints, that the soul by keeping in mind the commandments might train itself on the example of their zeal. He counselled them above all to ever bear in mind the Apostle's word, *Let not the sun go down upon your wrath,*[189] and to regard this as spoken of all the commandments alike: the sun must not go down, not merely on our anger, but on any other sin of ours. "It is but right and necessary, too, that the sun does not condemn us for any sin by day, nor the moon for any fault or even any thought by night. To assure ourselves of this, it is well to hear and treasure what the Apostle says: *Judge yourselves and prove yourselves.*[190] Wherefore, let every man daily take an accounting with himself of the day's and the night's doings; [191] and if he has sinned, let him stop sinning; and if he has not, let him not boast of it. Let him rather persist in the good and not grow careless, nor pass judgment on his neighbor, nor pronounce himself as just, as the blessed Apostle Paul said, *until the Lord comes who searches out the hidden things.*[192] For often we are not aware of what we are doing—we do not know it, but the Lord notices everything. Therefore, leaving judgment to Him, let us have sympathy with each other and *bear one another's burdens.*[193] Ourselves let us judge; and where we fall short, let us be earnest about making up our deficiency. Let this observation be a safeguard against sinning: let us each note and write down our actions and impulses of the soul as though we were to report them to each other; and you may rest assured that from utter

shame of becoming known we shall stop sinning and en-
tertaining sinful thoughts altogether. Who is there that
likes to be seen sinning? Who, having sinned, would not
choose to lie, hoping to escape detection? Just as we
would not give ourselves over to lust within sight of each
other, so if we were to write down our thoughts as if
telling them to each other, we shall so much the more
guard ourselves against foul thoughts for shame of being
known. Now, then, let the written account stand for the
eyes of our fellow ascetics, so that blushing at writing the
same as if we were actually seen, we may never ponder
evil. Molding ourselves in this way, we shall be able *to
bring our body into subjection,*[194] to please the Lord and
to trample under foot the machinations of the Enemy."

MIRACLES IN THE DESERT

56. Such were his words of advice to those who visited
him. With those who suffered he united in sympathy and
prayer; and often and in a great variety of cases the Lord
heard his prayer. But he neither boasted when he was
heard, nor did he complain when not heard. He always
gave thanks to the Lord, and urged the sufferers to bear
up and realize that healing was not his prerogative nor
indeed any man's, but God's who performs it when He
will and for whom He will. The sufferers were satisfied
to receive even the mere words of the old man as a cure,
for they had taken the lesson not to give up, but to be
long-suffering. And those who were cured learned not to
thank Antony, but God alone.

57. There was, for example, a man named Fronto,[195] hailing from Palatium. He had a dreadful disease, for he was continually biting his tongue, and his eyesight was failing. He came to the mountain and asked Antony to pray for him. The latter prayed and then said to Fronto: "Go, and you will be cured." But he was persistent and remained there for days, while Antony kept on saying: "You cannot be healed as long as you remain here. Go, and when you arrive in Egypt, you will see the miracle worked on you." The man was convinced and left; and the moment he came in sight of Egypt, his malady was gone. He was well according to the instructions of Antony which he had learned from the Savior in prayer.

58. A girl from Busiris in Tripoli [196] had a dreadful and very loathsome disease—a discharge from her eyes, nose, and ears immediately became worms when it fell to the ground. Moreover, her body was paralyzed and her eyes were defective. Her parents hearing of monks who were leaving to see Antony, and having faith in the Lord who healed the woman troubled with an issue of blood,[197] they asked to go along with their daughter. They consented. The parents and their child remained at the foot of the mountain with Paphnutius,[198] the confessor and monk. The others went up; and just as they wished to tell about the girl, he anticipated them and told them all about the sufferings of the child, and how she had made the journey with them.[199] Then when they asked if these people also might come in, he would not allow it, but said: "Go, and you will find her cured if she has not died. This certainly is no accomplishment of mine that she should come to a wretched man like me; no, indeed, her cure is the work of the Savior who shows His mercy in every

place to those who call upon Him. In this case, too, the Lord has granted her prayer, and His love for men has revealed to me that He will cure the child's malady where she is." At all events, the miracle actually took place: when they went down, they found the parents rejoicing and the girl in sound health from then on.

59. It happened that when two of the brethren were journeying to him, the water gave out on the journey: the one died and the other was on the point of dying. He no longer had strength to go, but lay on the ground expecting to die also. Antony, sitting on the mountain, called two monks who happened to be there, and urged them to hasten, saying: "Take a jar of water and run down the road towards Egypt; for two were coming, one has just died, and the other will unless you hurry. This has just now been revealed to me as I was praying." The monks, therefore, went and found the one lying dead and buried him. The other they revived with water and brought him to the old man. The distance was a day's journey. Now, if anyone asks why he did not speak before the other man died, his question is not justified. For the decree of death was not passed by Antony, but by God who determined it for the one and revealed the condition of the other. As for Antony, this alone was wonderful, that as he sat with sober heart on the mountain, the Lord showed him things afar off.

60. Again, on another occasion as he was sitting on the mountain and looking up, he saw in the air someone borne aloft amid great rejoicing of others who met him. Wondering at such a great host and thinking how blessed they were, he prayed to learn what this might be. And at

THE LIFE OF SAINT ANTONY

once a voice came to him saying that this was the soul of
the monk Amoun in Nitria.[200] He had lived the life of
an ascetic up to old age. Now, the distance from Nitria
to the mountain where Antony was takes thirteen days
to travel. Those who were with Antony, seeing the old
man in wonderment, asked what it meant and were told
that Amoun had just died.[201]

He was well-known, for he came there often and many
miracles had taken place through him. The following is
an example: Once when he had to cross the so-called
Lycus River [202] and it was the flood season, he asked Theodore [203] to go well ahead of him so that they might not
see each other naked while swimming across the water.
Then, when Theodore had gone off, he felt further shame
to see himself naked. While he was thus embarrassed and
pondering, he was suddenly borne across to the opposite
bank. Theodore, himself a pious man, came up; and
seeing that the other had come over before him and had
not even gotten wet, he asked how he had crossed. When
he saw that he did not wish to tell him, he clung to his
feet and insisted that he would not let him go until he
had learned this from him. Noting Theodore's determination, especially from the declaration he had made, he insisted in turn that he should not tell anyone till his death,
and so revealed to him that he had been carried across
and set down on the other side; that he had not walked
on the water and that this was not possible at all for
man, but for the Lord alone and for those whom He per-
mits, as He had done in the case of the great Apostle
Peter.[204] Theodore, then, told this after Amoun's death.

Now, the monks to whom Antony had spoken of
Amoun's death made a note of the day; and when after

thirty days the brethren arrived from Nitria, they inquired and learned that Amoun had fallen asleep [205] on that same day and hour when Antony saw his soul borne on high. And they as well as the others were amazed at the purity of Antony's soul, that he should learn at once what happened thirteen days away and should see the soul borne aloft.

61. Again, the count Archelaus [206] once met him in the Outer Mountain and asked him only to pray for Polycratia, [207] the admirable Christ-bearing [208] virgin of Laodicea. She was suffering severely from her stomach and side because of her excessive austerity, and her body was in an utterly weakened condition. Antony prayed, and the count made a note of the day on which the prayer was made. When he returned to Laodicea, he found the virgin well. Inquiring when and on what day she had been freed from her sickness, he produced the paper on which he had marked the time of the prayer. When he had been told, he immediately showed his notation on the paper; and all were astonished as they recognized that the Lord had cured her of her ailment at the very moment when Antony was praying and appealing to the Savior's goodness on her behalf.

62. And as for those who came to him, he frequently foretold their coming, days and sometimes a month in advance and for what reason they were coming. Some came merely to see him, others through sickness, and others suffering from demons. And all thought the exertion of the journey no trouble or loss: each returned feeling that he had been helped. While Antony had these powers of speech and vision, yet he begged that no one

should admire him for this account, but rather admire the
Lord, because He granted to us mere men to know Him
to the best of our capability.

63. On another occasion he had again come down to
visit the outer cells. When he had been invited to enter a
ship and pray with the monks, he alone perceived a hor-
rible, very biting smell. The crew said that there were fish
and salted meat on board and the odor was from them,
but he insisted that the smell was different. While he
was still speaking, a young man who had a demon and
had come on board earlier as a stowaway, suddenly let
out a shriek. On being censured in the name of our Lord
Jesus Christ, the demon went out and the man became
normal; and all knew that the stench was from the demon.

64. And another, a man of rank, came to him possessed by a demon. In this case the demon was so frightful
that the possessed [209] man was not aware that he was
going to Antony. He even devoured the excrement of his
own body. The men who brought him begged Antony to
pray for him. Feeling compassion for the young man,
Antony prayed and kept awake with him the whole night.
Towards dawn the youth suddenly rushed upon Antony
and gave him a push. His companions became vexed at
this, but Antony said: "Do not be angry with the young
man, for he is not responsible, but the demon in him.
Being rebuked and commanded to be gone to waterless
places,[210] he was driven mad and he did this. Give thanks
to the Lord, therefore, for his attacking me in this way is
a sign of the demon's departure." The moment Antony
had said this, the young man was normal again. Restored
to his senses, he recognized where he was and embraced
the old man, giving thanks to God.

VISIONS

65. Numerous monks have stories—stories uniformly concordant—about many other such things done through him. These, however, do not appear so marvellous as compared with still more marvellous things. Once, for example, when he was about to eat and stood up to pray, about the ninth hour,[211] he felt himself carried off in spirit, and—strange to say—as he stood he saw himself, as it were, outside himself [212] and as though guided aloft by certain beings. Then he also saw loathsome and terrible beings standing in the air and bent on preventing him from passing through.[213] As his guides offered resistance, the others demanded to know on what plea he was not accountable to them. Then, when they set themselves to taking an account from his birth, Antony's guides intervened, saying to them: "As for the things dating from his birth, the Lord has erased them; but as for the time since he became monk and promised himself to God, you can take an account." Then, as they brought accusations but could not prove them, the way opened up to him free and unhindered; and presently he saw himself approaching, so it seemed to him, and halting with himself; and so he was the real Antony again.

Then, forgetting to eat, he spent the rest of the day and all the night sighing and praying. For he was astonished to see against how many we battle and what labors a person has to pass through the air; and he remembered that this is what the Apostle said—*according to the prince*

of the power of the air.[214] Here precisely lies the Enemy's
power, that he fights and tries to stop those who pass
through. Wherefore, too, his special admonition: *Take
unto you the armor of God that you may be able to resist
in the evil day . . . ;* [215] *that having no evil to say of us the
Enemy may be put to shame.*[216] And we who have learned
this, let us remember what the Apostle says: *Whether in
the body I know not, or out of the body I know not; God
knoweth.*[217] But Paul was carried up to the third heaven
and heard *words unutterable* [218] and returned; whereas
Antony saw himself entering the air and struggling until
he became free.

66. Again, he had this favor from God. When he sat
alone on the mountain, if ever in his reflections he failed
to find a solution, it was revealed to him by Providence
in answer to his prayer: the happy man was, in the words
of Scripture, *taught of God.*[219] Thus favored, he once had
had a discussion with some visitors about the life of the
soul and the kind of place it will have after this life. The
following night there came a call from on high saying,
"Antony, rise, go out and look!" He went out, therefore—
he knew which calls to heed [220]—and, looking up, saw a
towering figure, unsightly and frightening, standing and
reaching to the clouds; further, certain beings ascending
as though on wings. The former was stretching out his
hands: some of the latter were stopped by him, while
others flew over him and, having come through, rose without further trouble. At such as these the monster gnashed
his teeth, but exulted over those who fell. Forthwith a
voice addressed itself to Antony, *"Understand the
vision!"* [221] .His understanding opened up,[222] and he real-

ized that it was the passing of souls [223] and that the
monster standing there was the Enemy, the envier of the
faithful. Those answerable to him he lays hold of and
keeps them from passing through, but those whom he
failed to win over he cannot master as they pass out of
his range. Here again, having seen this and taking it as a
reminder, he struggled the more to advance from day to
day in the things that lay before him.

He was not inclined to tell about these things to people.
But when he had spent a long time in prayer and the
wonder of it all absorbed him, and his companions kept
on inquiring about it and importuning him, he was forced
to speak. As a father he could not keep the secret from his
children. He felt that his own conscience was clear and
to tell them this might be a help to them. They would
learn of the good fruit that the ascetic life brings and that
often visions are granted as a compensation for its
hardships.

ANTONY'S DEVOTION TO THE CHURCH'S
MINISTERS

67. He was, moreover, forbearing by disposition and
humble of soul. Renowned man that he was, he yet
showed the profoundest respect for the Church's ministry and he wanted every cleric [225] to be honored above
himself. [226] He was not ashamed to bow his head before
bishops and priests; and if ever a deacon came to him for
help, he conversed with him on what was helpful; but
when it came to prayers, he would ask him to lead, not

being ashamed to learn himself. In fact, he would often ask questions and seek the views of his companions; and if he profited from what another said, he made acknowledgement of it.

His face, too, had a great and indescribable charm in it. And he had this added gift from the Savior: if he was present in a gathering of monks and someone who had no previous acquaintance with him wished to see him, as soon as he arrived he would pass over the others and run to Antony as if drawn by his eyes. It was not his stature or figure that made him stand out from the rest, but his settled character and the purity of his soul. For his soul was imperturbed, and so his outward appearance was calm.[227] The joy in his soul expressed itself in the cheerfulness of his face, and from the body's behavior one saw and knew the state of his soul, as Scripture says: *When the heart is glad, the face is radiant; but when it is full of grief, the face is gloomy.*[228] Thus Jacob observed that Laban was plotting against him, and said to his wives: *Your father's countenance is not as yesterday and the day before.*[229] Thus Samuel recognized David, for he had eyes that begot gladness and teeth white as milk.[230] So, too, was Antony recognized: he was never agitated, for his soul was calm; he was never gloomy, for there was joy in his mind.

HIS LOYALTY TO THE FAITH

68. Again, in matters of faith his devotion was absolutely admirable. For instance, he never had anything to do with the Meletian [231] schismatics, aware of their wick-

edness and apostasy from the beginning. Nor did he have
any friendly dealings with the Manichaeans [232] or any
other heretics, except only to admonish them to return to
the true religion.[233] He thought and taught that friend-
ship and association with them brought harm and ruin
to the soul. So, too, he loathed the heresy of the Arians [234]
and he exhorted all not to go near them nor to share their
perverted belief. Once when some of the Ariomaniacs [235]
came to him, he questioned them closely; and when he
learned of their impious faith, he drove them from the
mountain, saying that their words were worse than the
poison of serpents.

69. When on one occasion the Arians gave out the lie
that his views were the same as theirs, he showed that he
was vexed and angry with them. Answering the appeal
of both the bishops and all the brethren, he came down
from the mountain, and entering Alexandria,[236] he de-
nounced the Arians. He said that their heresy was the
worst of all and a forerunner of the Antichrist. He taught
the people that the Son of God is not a creature nor has
He come into being "from non-existence"; but "He is the
eternal Word and Wisdom of the substance of the Father.
Hence, too, it is impious to say, 'there was a time when He
was not,' [237] for the Word was always coexistent with the
Father. Wherefore, do not have the least thing to do with
the most godless Arians: there simply is no *fellowship of
light with darkness*.[238] You must remember that you are
God-fearing Christians, but they by saying that the Son
and Word of God the Father is a creature, are in no respect different from the pagans *who worship the created
in place of God the Creator*.[239] And you may be sure that

all creation is incensed against them because they count among created things the Creator and Lord of all, to whom all things owe their existence."

70. The people all rejoiced to hear such a man anathematize the heresy which fights against Christ.[240]   The entire city ran together to see Antony. Pagans,[241] too, and even their so-called priests came to the church saying: "We would like to see the man of God"—for so they all called him. Moreover, there also the Lord through him rid many of demons and cured mental cases. Many pagans, too, asked but to touch the old man, confident that they would be helped; and, indeed, as many became Christians in those few days as one would have seen in a year. Again, some thought he was annoyed by the crowds and therefore were trying to keep all away from him; but he, unannoyed, said: "These people are no more numerous than those demons we wrestle with on the mountain."

71. When he was leaving and we [242] were seeing him off and had arrived at the gate, a woman behind us cried out: "Wait, man of God, my daughter is terribly plagued by a demon! Wait, please, or I shall hurt myself running." The old man heard her, we begged him to stop, and he did so gladly. When the woman approached, her child was hurled to the ground. Antony prayed and called upon the name of Christ, the child stood up cured as the unclean spirit left her. The mother gave praise to God and all gave thanks. And he, too, rejoiced as he left for the mountain—to him his own home.[243]

WISDOM TO THE WISE

72. He also had a very high degree of practical wisdom. The wonder was that although he was without formal schooling,[244] he was yet a man of ready wit and understanding. To illustrate: once two Greek philosophers came to him, thinking they could experiment with Antony. He happened to be on the Outer Mountain at the time. When he had sized up the men from their appearance, he went out to them and said through an interpreter: "Why, philosophers, have you gone to so much trouble to come to a foolish man?" When they said that he was not foolish, but very wise, he said to them: "If you have come to a foolish man, your trouble is to no purpose; but if you do think that I am wise, make yourselves what I am, for one ought to imitate the good. Indeed, if I had come to you, I would have imitated you; conversely, now that you have come to me, make yourselves what I am: I am a Christian." They left marvelling at him, for they saw that even demons feared Antony.

73. Others again of the same kind met him in the Outer Mountain and thought they could fop him because he had not received any schooling. Antony said to them: "Well, what do you say, which is first, the mind or letters? And which is the cause of which—the mind of letters, or letters of the mind?" When they stated that the mind is first and the inventor of letters, Antony said: "Therefore, one who has a sound mind has no need of letters." [245] This amazed both them and the bystanders. They went away

astonished to see such wisdom in an ordinary man.[246] For he did not have the rough manner of one who had lived and grown old in the mountains, but he was a man of grace and urbanity. His speech was seasoned with divine wisdom [247] so that no one bore him ill-will, but rather all rejoiced over him who sought him out.

74. And indeed, after this still others came.[248] They were of those who among the pagans are supposedly wise. They asked him to state an argument for our faith in Christ. When they tried to make inferences from the preaching of the divine Cross [249] and wished to scoff, Antony paused for a moment, and first pitying them for their ignorance, said through an interpreter who gave an excellent translation of his words: "Which is better—to confess the Cross, or to attribute adulteries and pederasties to your so-called gods? For to maintain what we maintain is a sign of manly spirit and betokens disregard for death, whereas your claims bespeak but wanton passions. Again, which is better—to say that the Word of God was not changed, but remaining the same took on a human body for the salvation and well-being of mankind, so that by sharing human birth, He might make men partakers of the divine and spiritual nature; [250] or to put the divine on a level with senseless things and therefore to worship beasts and reptiles and images of men? These precisely are the objects worshipped by you wise men. How dare you revile us for saying that Christ has appeared as man, whereas you derive the soul from heaven, saying that it strayed and fell from the vault of the heavens into the body? Would that it were only into the body of man, and not that it changed and migrated into beasts and serpents! [251]

Our faith declares Christ's coming [252] for the salvation of men; but you mistakenly theorize about an uncreated Soul.[253] We believe in the power of Providence and His love of men and that this [254] also was not impossible with God; but you, calling the Soul an image of the Mind,[255] impute falls to it and fabricate myths about its ability to change.[256] Consequently, you make also the Mind itself changeable because of the Soul. For as was the image, so, too, must be that of which it is the image. But when you have such thoughts about the Mind, remember that you are also blaspheming the Father of the Mind.[257]

75. "And regarding the Cross, which would you say is better: when treachery is resorted to by wicked men, to endure the Cross and not to flinch from death in any manner or form,[258] or to fabricate fables about the wanderings of Osiris and Isis,[259] the plots of Typhon, the banishment of Cronus,[260] the swallowing of children, and slaying of fathers? Yes, here we have your wisdom!

"And why is it that while you deride the Cross, you do not marvel at the Resurrection? For those who reported the one also wrote of the other. Or why is it that while you remember the Cross, you have nothing to say about the dead brought back to life, the blind who saw again, the paralytics who were cured and the lepers made clean, the walking on the sea, and the other signs and wonders which show Christ not as man but as God? At all events, it seems to me that you are but defrauding yourselves and are not really familiar with our Scriptures. But do read them and see that the things which Christ did, prove Him to be God abiding with us for the salvation of mankind.

76. "But you must also tell us your own teachings.

Though, what could you say about senseless things except senselessness and barbarism? But if, as I hear, you wish to say that among you people such things are spoken figuratively; [261] and you make the rape of Persephone [262] an allegory of the earth, Hephaestus' lameness of the fire, Hera of the air, Apollo of the sun, Artemis of the moon, and Poseidon of the sea: even so you are not worshipping God Himself, but you are rendering service to the creature in place of the God who created all. For if you have composed such stories because creation is beautiful, it was for you to go no further than to admire it, and not to make gods of the creatures lest you give the honor that is the Maker's [263] to the things made. In that case it were time that you transferred the honor due the architect to the house built by him, or the honor due the general to the soldier. Now, what have you to say to all this? Thus we shall know whether the Cross has anything that deserves to be made a jest of."

77. They were embarrassed and turning this way and that. Antony smiled and said, again through an interpreter: "Sight itself bears proof of all that I have said. But since, of course, you pin your faith on demonstrative proofs and this is an art in which you are masters, and you want us also not to worship God without demonstrative arguments—do you first tell me this. How does precise knowledge of things come about, especially knowledge about God? Is it by verbal proof or by an act of faith? And which comes first, an active faith or verbal proof?" When they replied that the act of faith takes precedence and that this constitutes accurate knowledge, Antony said: "Well said! Faith arises from the disposition of the soul, while dialectic comes from the skill of those who

devise it. Accordingly, those who are equipped with an active faith have no need of verbal argument, and probably find it even superfluous. For what we apprehend by faith, that you attempt to construct by arguments; and often you cannot even express what we perceive. The conclusion is that an active faith is better and stronger than your sophistic arguments.

78. "We Christians, therefore, possess religious truth [264] not on the basis of Greek philosophical reasoning,[265] but founded on the power of a faith vouchsafed us by God through Jesus Christ. And as for the truth of the account given, note how we who have remained unlettered believe in God, recognizing from His works His Providence over all things. And as for our faith being something effectual, note how we lean upon our belief in Christ, while you take support from sophistical wranglings over words; and your phantom idols are passing into desuetude, but our faith is spreading everywhere. And you with your syllogisms and sophisms are not converting anybody from Christianity to paganism; [266] but we, teaching faith in Christ, are stripping your gods of the fear they inspired,[267] now that all are recognizing Christ as God and the Son of God. You with all your elegant diction do not hinder the teaching of Christ; but we by mentioning the name of the crucified Christ drive away all the demons whom you fear as gods. Where the Sign of the Cross appears, there magic is powerless and sorcery ineffectual.[268]

79. "Indeed, tell us, where are now your oracles? Where are the incantations of the Egyptians? Where are the phantom illusions of the magicians? When did all these things cease and lose their significance? Was it not

when the Cross of Christ came? Wherefore, is it this that
deserves scorn, and not rather the things that have been
done away with by it and proved powerless? This, too, is
remarkable, the fact that your religion was never persecuted; on the contrary, among men it is held in honor in
every city. Christ's followers, however, are persecuted,
and yet it is our cause that flourishes and prevails, not
yours. Your religion, for all the tranquillity and protection
it enjoys, is dying; whereas the faith and teaching of
Christ, scorned by you and often persecuted by the rulers,
has filled the world. When was there a time that the
knowledge of God shone forth so brightly? Or when was
there a time that continence and the virtue of virginity so
showed itself? Or when was death so despised as when the
Cross of Christ came? And this no one doubts when he
sees [269] the martyrs despising death for Christ's sake, or
sees the virgins of the Church who for Christ's sake keep
their bodies pure and undefiled.

80. "These are proofs sufficient to show that faith in
Christ is the only true religion. Still, here you are—you
who seek for conclusions based on reasoning, you have no
faith! We, however, do not prove, as our teacher said, *in
persuasive words of Greek wisdom;* [270] but it is by faith that
we persuade men, faith which tangibly precedes any con-
structive reasoning of arguments. See, here we have with
us some who are suffering from demons." These were
people who had come to him troubled by demons; bringing
them forward, he said: "Either cleanse these by your
syllogisms and by any art or magic you wish, calling on
your idols; or, if you cannot, then stop fighting us and see
the power of the Cross of Christ." Having said this, he
invoked Christ and signed the afflicted with the Sign of the

Cross, repeating the action a second and third time. And at once the persons stood up completely cured, restored to their right mind and giving thanks to the Lord. The so-called philosophers were astonished and really amazed at the man's sagacity and at the miracle performed. But Antony said: "Why do you marvel at this? It is not we who do it, but Christ who does these things through those who believe in Him. Do you, therefore, also believe, and you will see that it is not wordcraft which we have, but faith through love that works for Christ; and if you, too, will make this your own, you will no longer seek arguments from reason, but will consider faith in Christ sufficient by itself."

So did Antony speak. They admired him as they left, embraced him and acknowledged that they had been helped by him.

THE EMPEROR CONSTANTINE
WRITES TO HIM

81. The fame of Antony reached even to emperors; for when Constantine Augustus and his sons Constantius Augustus and Constans Augustus heard about these things, they wrote [271] to him as to a father and begged him to write back. He, however, did not make much of the documents nor did he rejoice over the letters; but he was the same as he was before the emperor wrote to him. When the documents were brought to him, he called the monks and said: "You must not be surprised if an emperor writes to us, for he is a man; but you should rather be

surprised that God has written the law for mankind and
has spoken to us through His own Son." [272] Indeed, he did
not like to accept the letters, saying that he did not know
what to answer to such things. But being persuaded by
the monks who urged that the emperors were Christians
and that they might take offense at being ignored, he had
them read. And he wrote back, commending them for
worshipping Christ, and giving them salutary advice not
to think highly of the things of this world, but rather to
bear in mind the judgment to come; and to know that
Christ alone is the true and eternal King.[273] He begged
them to show themselves humane and to have a regard for
justice and for the poor. And they were glad to receive
his answer. So was he beloved by all, and all wished to
have him as a father.

HE FORETELLS THE RAVAGES
OF THE ARIAN HERETICS

82. Giving such account of himself and thus answering
those who sought him out, he returned again to the Inner
Mountain. He kept up his wonted ascetic practices, and
often as he was sitting or walking with visitors he would
become dumb, as it is written in Daniel.[274] After some
time he would take up again what he had been saying to
the brethren who were with him; and those present would
know that he was seeing a vision. For often when he was
on the mountain he saw things happening even in Egypt.
He would describe them to the bishop Serapion [275] when
he chanced to be on the Inner Mountain [276] and saw
Antony entranced in a vision.

On one occasion, for instance, as he sat working, he took on the appearance of one in ecstasy. and moaned continuously at what he saw. Then after some time he turned to those present, moaning and trembling, and prayed and knelt down, remaining in that position a long time. And when he arose, the old man was weeping. Then those with him were shaken and very much alarmed and asked him to tell what it was; and they pressed him for a long time until he was constrained to speak. Sighing deeply, he said: "Oh, my children, it were better to die before the things in the vision take place." When they asked further questions, he said with tears: "Wrath is about to strike the Church and she is about to be delivered up to men who are like to senseless beasts. For I saw the table of the Lord's house, and mules around it standing on all sides in a ring and kicking up their hoofs at what was within, the same as the kicking you have when a frisking herd runs wild. You surely heard," he said, "how I moaned; I heard a voice saying: 'My altar shall be desecrated.' "

So spoke the old man; and two years later came the present assault of the Arians and the plundering of the churches,[77] when they took the vessels by force and had them carried away by the pagans; when, too, they forced the pagans from the shops to their meetings and in their presence did as they pleased on the sacred table. Then we all realized that the kicking of the mules presaged to Antony what the Arians are now doing like so many senseless beasts.

When he saw this vision, he consoled his companions, saying: "Do not be discouraged, children, for as the Lord has been angry, so will He bring us recovery later. And the Church will quickly regain the beauty that is hers and shine with her wonted splendor. You will see the persecuted restored and irreligion retreating again to its proper haunts and the true faith asserting itself every-where with complete freedom. Only, do not defile yourselves with the Arians. This their teaching is not of the Apostles, but of the demons and their father, the Devil. Indeed, it is sterile and unreasonable, and it lacks right sense—like the senselessness of mules." [278]

GOD'S WONDER-WORKER AND PHYSICIAN OF SOULS

83. Such is the story of Antony. We must not show ourselves skeptical when it is through a man that all these great wonders came to pass. For it is the promise of the Savior who says: *If you have faith as a grain of mustard seed, you shall say to this mountain: 'Remove hence!' and it shall remove; and nothing shall be impossible to you.*[279] And again: *Amen, amen, I say to you, if you ask the Father anything in my name, He will give it to you . . . . Ask and you shall receive.*[280] And it is He who said to His disciples and to all who believe in Him: *Heal the sick; . . . cast out the demons; freely have you received, freely give.*[281]

84. Antony, then, healed not by giving out commands, but by praying and by calling upon Christ's name, so that it was clear to all that it was not he who did this, but the Lord showing His loving-kindness to men and curing the sufferers through Antony. Antony had to do only with

prayer and the practice of asceticism for the sake of which he lived his mountain life, happy in the contemplation of the divine and grieving that many disturbed him and forced him to the Outer Mountain.

All the judges, for instance, begged him to come down from the mountain, since it was impossible for them to go there because of their following of people involved in lawsuits. They asked him to come that they might but see him. But he tried to avoid the journey to them and begged to be excused from making it. They persisted, however, and even sent to him defendants under escort of soldiers, that on account of these he might come down. Under such compulsion, therefore, and seeing them lamenting, he would go to the Outer Mountain; and again the trouble he went to was not in vain, for to many he was a help and his coming a benefaction. He helped the judges by counselling them to give justice precedence over all else, and to fear God and to bear in mind *with what judgment they judged they would be judged*.[282] But of all things he loved his mountain life most.

85. Once when he had been thus importuned by persons who needed assistance and the military commander had sent numerous messengers asking him to come down, he came and spoke a few words on the subject of salvation and in behalf of those who wanted him, and then hastened to leave. When the duke,[283] as he is called, begged him to stay, he said he could not spend any time with them, and satisfied him by a beautiful comparison, saying: "Just as fish exposed for any length of time on dry land die, so monks go to pieces when they loiter among you and spend too much time with you. Therefore, we must off to the mountain, as fish to the sea. Other-

wise, if we tarry, we may lose sight of the inner life."
The commandant on hearing this and much more from
him, admiringly said that truly this was a servant of God;
for whence could an ordinary man have such extraordinary intelligence, unless he were beloved of God?

86. There was one commandant—Balacius was his
name—[284] who in his partisanship for the execrable Arians
bitterly persecuted us Christians. And since he was so
barbaric as to beat virgins and strip and flog monks,[285]
Antony sent him a letter with the following contents:
"I see God's judgment aproaching you; stop, therefore,
persecuting Christians, that the judgment may not seize
you; even now it is on the point of overtaking you." But
Balacius laughed, threw the letter on the ground and spat
on it, and maltreated the bearers, telling them to take
back this message to Antony: "Seeing that you are concerned about the monks, I shall now come after you, too."
And five days had not passed when God's judgment over-
took him. For Balacius and Nestorius, the prefect of
Egypt,[286] had gone out to the first station out of Alexandria,
which is called Chereu,[287] and both were on horseback. The
horses belonged to Balacius and were the most gentle of
all he kept. They had not yet reached the place, when the
horses began to frisk with one another, as horses do, and
suddenly the gentler of the two, the one on which
Nestorius was riding, bit Balacius, threw him down, and
attacked him; and it rent his thigh so badly with its teeth,
that he had to be taken back to the city at once and he
died in three days. And all wondered that what Antony
had foretold was fulfilled so quickly.

87. Thus did he warn the harsh. But as for the others

who came to him, his heart-to-heart talks with them made them forthwith forget their litigation and deem those happy who withdraw from life in the world. He so championed the cause of the wronged that one would think that he himself, not the others, was the injured party. Further, he had such a gift for helping everybody that many who were in military service and many men of great affluence gave up their burdensome life and then became monks. In a word, it was as though a physician had been given by God to Egypt. For who came to him in grief and did not return in joy? Who came weeping for his dead and did not immediately put away his mourning? Who came in anger and was not transformed into friendliness? What down-and-out pauper met him, and seeing him and hearing him did not despise wealth and feel consoled in his poverty? What monk grown careless did not gain new fervor from a visit with him? What young man coming to the mountain, and seeing Antony, did not promptly renounce pleasure and love chastity? Who came to him plagued by a demon and was not freed? Who came with tortured mind and did not find peace of mind?

88. This was also unique in Antony's practice of asceticism that, as I stated above, he had the gift of discerning spirits.[288] He recognized their movements and was well aware in what direction each of them directed his effort and attack. Not only was he himself not fooled by them, but encouraging others who were harassed in their thoughts, he taught them how they might ward off their designs, describing the weaknesses and wiles of the spirits practicing possession. And so each went down as though anointed [289] by him and filled with confidence against the designs of the Devil and his demons.

And how many girls who had suitors but who had seen
Antony only from afar, remained virgins for Christ!
People came to him also from foreign lands. These received help like all the others, and returned as though sent
on their way by a father. And indeed, now that he has
passed away, all, like orphans who have lost their father,
comfort themselves by one thing—their memory of him—
cherishing at the same time his words of admonition and
counsel.

DEATH

89. This is also the place for me to tell and for you to
hear, as you are anxious to, how he came to the end of his
life; for in this, too, he was a model for imitation.

As was his wont, he happened to be visiting the monks
in the Outer Mountain. Receiving a premonition of his
death from Providence, he spoke to the brethren, saying:
"This is the last visit I am making with you, and I am
wondering if we shall see each other again in this life.
It is time now for me to die, for I am near a hundred and
five years." Hearing this they wept, embracing and kissing
the old man. But he, as though he were departing from
a foreign town for his own, chatted joyously. He exhorted
them "not to grow lax in their efforts nor to lose heart in
the practice of the ascetic life, but to live as though dying
daily; and, as I have said before, to work hard to guard
the soul from filthy thoughts; to emulate holy men. Do
not go near the Meletian schismatics, for you know their
wicked and unholy teaching. Have nothing to do with
the Arians, for the irreligion of these is plain to everyone.

And if you should see the judges supporting them, you must not permit yourself to be confused: this will come to an end—it is a phenomenon that is mortal and bound to last for but a short time. Therefore, keep yourselves clean from these and watch over the tradition of the Fathers, and, above all, the orthodox faith in our Lord Jesus Christ, as you have learned it from the Scriptures and as you have often been put in mind of by me."

90. When the brethren urged him to stay with them and die there, he refused to do so for many reasons, as he indicated, though without saying anything, and especially because of this. The Egyptians have the custom of honoring with funeral rites and wrapping in linen shrouds the bodies of good men, and especially of the holy martyrs; but they do not bury them in the earth, but place them on couches and keep them with them at home, thinking in this way to honor the departed. Antony had often asked even the bishops to give instructions to the people on the matter. Likewise he had made laymen ashamed and reproved women, saying that this was "not right nor reverent at all. The bodies of the Patriarchs and the Prophets are preserved in tombs to this day; and the body of the Lord, too, was placed in a tomb, and a stone set there hid it [290] until He rose on the third day." By stating the case thus, he showed that he commits a wrong who after death does not bury the bodies of the departed, holy though they be. Indeed, what is greater or holier than the Lord's body? As a result, many who had heard him, from then on buried their dead [291] and thanked the Lord that they had received a good lesson.

91. He knew this and was afraid that they might do

the same to his own body. Therefore, bidding farewell to
the monks on the Outer Mountain, he hastily made for
the Inner Mountain where he was used to living. After
a few months he fell sick. He called those who were with
him—there were two there who had been ascetics for
fifteen years and looked after him because of his great age [292]
—and said to them: "I am going the way of my fathers, as
Scripture says,[293] for I see myself called by the Lord.
And you—be on your guard and do not bring to naught the
asceticism you have practiced for so long. Make it your
endeavor to keep up your enthusiasm as though you were
but now beginning. You know the demons and their
designs, you know how fierce they are, yet how powerless.
So, do not fear them; rather, let Christ be your life's
breath, and place your confidence in Him. Live as if dying
daily,[294] taking heed for yourselves and remembering the
counsels you have heard from me. Let there be no com-
munion whatever between you and the schismatics and
none at all with the heretical Arians.[295] You know how
I myself have kept away from them because of their
Christ-attacking false heresy. Show your eagerness to
give your allegiance, first to the Lord and then to His
saints, *that after your death they may receive you into
everlasting dwellings* [296] as familiar friends. Give these
things your thought, make them your purpose; and if you
have any care for me and think of me as a father, do not
allow anyone to take my body into Egypt, lest they should
keep it in their houses. This was my reason for going
to the mountain and coming here. You know how I have
always put to shame those who do this and charged them
to stop the custom. Therefore, carry out my obsequies
yourselves and bury my body in the earth and let what

I have said be so respected by you, that no one will know the place but you alone. At the resurrection of the dead I shall receive it back from the Savior incorruptible. Distribute my garments. To Bishop Athanasius give the one sheepskin and the cloak on which I lie, which he gave me but which has worn out in my possession; [297] and to Bishop Serapion give the other sheepskin, and keep the hair shirt for yourselves. And now, my children, God bless you; Antony is going and is with you no more."

92. Having said this and having been kissed by them, he drew up his feet; and with a look as though friends had come to him and he was overjoyed at sight of them—for, as he lay there, his face had a cheerful look—he passed away and was gathered to his fathers. Then they, following the orders he had given them, prepared and wrapped up the body and buried it there in the earth. And to this day no one knows where he is buried, save those two only.[298] As for the recipients of the sheepskin of the blessed Antony and the cloak worn out by him, each guards his gift as some great treasure. For to look on them is like seeing Antony; and to wear them is like taking on his exhortations with joy.

93. This was the end of Antony's life in the body, as above we had the beginning of his ascetical life. And though this be but a meagre account as compared with the virtue of the man, yet do take this and reflect what manner of man Antony, the man of God, was. From youth to so great an age he preserved an unswerving devotion to the ascetic life. He never made old age the excuse for yielding to the desire for lavish foods, nor did he change in his form of clothing because of his body's

infirmity, nor did he as much as wash his feet with water.
And yet his health remained entirely unimpaired. For
instance, even his eyes were perfectly normal so that his
sight was excellent; and he had not lost a single tooth,
only they had worn down near the gums through the old
man's great age. He also kept healthy hands and feet, and
on the whole he appeared brighter and more active than
did all those who use a diversified diet and baths and a
variety of clothing.

The fact that he became famous everywhere and that
he found universal admiration and his loss is felt even by
people who have never seen him, betokens his virtue and
a soul beloved of God. For Antony gained renown not
for his writings, nor for worldly wisdom, nor for any art,
but solely for his service of God.

And that this was something God-given no one could
deny. For whence was it that this man who lived hidden
in a mountain was heard of in Spain and Gaul, in Rome
and in Africa, if it was not God who everywhere makes
known His own, who, moreover, had told this to Antony
at the very beginning? [299] For though they do their work
in secret and though they wish to remain obscure, yet the
Lord shows them forth as lamps to all men, that thus
again those who hear of them may realize that the commandments can lead to perfection, and may take courage
on the path to virtue.

EPILOGUE

94. Now, then, read this to the other brethren,[300] that
they may learn what the life of monks should be like
and that they may be convinced that our Lord and Savior
Jesus Christ glorifies those who glorify Him; and that He
not only leads to the Kingdom of Heaven those who serve
Him to the end, but even here He makes them, though
they hide themselves and strive to live away from the
world, known and spoken of everywhere because of their
own goodness and because of the help they give to others.
And if the occasion presents itself, read it also to the
pagans, that at least in this way they may learn that our
Lord Jesus Christ is not only God and the Son of God,
but that the Christians by their faithful service to Him
and their orthodox faith in Him prove that the demons
whom the Greeks consider gods are no gods; that, moreover, they trample them under foot and drive them out
for what they are—deceivers and corrupters of men;
through Jesus Christ our Lord, to whom is glory for ever
and ever.   Amen.

NOTES

LIST OF ABBREVIATIONS

Acta SS   J. Bollandus (Bollandists), *Acta sanctorum* (Antwerp, etc. 1643-)

ACW   *Ancient Christian Writers* (Westminster, Md. 1946-)

Bardenhewer   O. Bardenhewer, *Geschichte der altkirchlichen Literatur* 1-3, 2nd ed.; 4-5 (1913-1932)

Butler   C. Butler, *The Lausiac History of Palladius* 1-2 (Texts and Studies 6. 1-2, Cambridge 1898-1904)

DACL   *Dictionnaire d'archéologie chrétienne et de liturgie* (Paris 1924-)

DTC   *Dictionnaire de théologie catholique* (Paris 1903-)

LTK   *Lexikon für Theologie und Kirche* 1-10 (Freiburg i. Br. 1930-1938)

MG   J. P. Migne, *Patrologia graeca*

OCD   *Oxford Classical Dictionary* (Oxford 1949)

RE   A. Pauly—G. Wissowa—W. Kroll, *Realenzyklopädie der classischen Altertumswissenschaft* (Stuttgart 1894-)

TWNT   G. Kittel, *Theologisches Wörterbuch zum Neuen Testament* (Stuttgart 1933-)

INTRODUCTION

[1] This was the common view in the fourth century—cf. St. Jerome, *Vita S. Pauli* 1. Some, whom Jerome favors, held that the title belonged to the hermit Paul of Thebes (228-341). See W. H. Mackean, *Christian Monasticism in Egypt to the Close of the Fourth Century* (London 1920) 67 f.

[2] Cf. Sozomen, *Hist. Eccl.* 1. 13, and below, n. 5 to the text.

[3] Matt. 19. 21.

⁴ *Ibid.* 6. 34.

⁵ 2 Thess. 3. 10.

⁶ Regarding certain chronological difficulties, notably the question whether or not the period spent in the tomb and the time he lived in the abandoned fort are concurrent or identical, cf. L. v. Hertling, *Antonius der Einsiedler* (Forsch. z. Gesch. d. innerkirchlichen Lebens 1, Innsbruck 1929) 30-34.

⁷ See below, § 12 of the text and n. 52.

⁸ See below, § 46 and nn. 163-7.

⁹ See below, n. 177 to the text.

¹⁰ C. Kingsley, *The Hermits* (London 1868) 128.

¹¹ Cf. Mackean, *op. cit.* 79 f.; P. F. Anson, *The Quest of Solitude* (London 1932) 16 f.

¹² Cf. St. Jerome, *Vita S. Hilar.* 3.

¹³ *Hist. monach. in Aegypto* 28 (86-90 Preuschen); Rufinus, *Apol. in Hier.* 2. 12.

¹⁴ Cf. *Hist. Laus.* 8 (2. 26-29 Butler), and below, § 60 with n. 200; for Paul the Simple, see *Hist. Laus.* 22 (2. 69-74 Butler).

¹⁵ Butler 1. 225 f.

¹⁶ Butler, the title entered above in the List of Abbreviations; Bousset, *Apophthegmata, Studien zur Geschichte des ältesten Mönchtums* (Tübingen 1923). For further literature, cf. B. Altaner's Italian edition (by A. Ferrua) of his patrology: *Patrologia* (Rome 1944) 146 f.; for the *Apophthegmata,* note E. C. Tappert, 'A Greek Hagiologic Manuscript in Philadelphia,' *Trans. of the Am. Philol. Assoc.* 68 (1937) 264-76. Generous samples of the *Verba Seniorum* and the *Historia Monachorum in Aegypto* were recently given in English translation by Miss Helen Waddell, *The Desert Fathers* (New York 1936) 53-216.

¹⁷ Some of these references and others occurring elsewhere have been incorporated in the observations on the text: cf. nn. 16, 60, 166, 170, 178, 236, 243, 246, 292, 297.

¹⁸ Following the studies of A. Eichhorn, *Athanasii de vita ascetica testimonia collecta* (Halle 1886). See below, n. 277 to the text.

¹⁹ Thus v. Hertling, *op. cit.* 7 n. 2, who favors the period when Athanasius finally resided in peace in Alexandria, 365-373.

²⁰ Cf. Butler 1. 215-28: 'Recent Theories Concerning St. Antony.'

²¹ St. Jerome, *De viris ill.* 87 f., 125.

²² St. Gregory Nazianzen, *Or. 21 (In laudem Athanasii)* 5.

²³ Palladius, *Hist. Laus.* 8 (2. 28 Butler).

[24] *Select Writings and Letters of Athanasius, Bishop of Alexandria*, in *A Select Library of Nicene and Post-Nicene Fathers of the Christian Church* 4 (New York-Oxford-London 1892) 188, where see his excellent summary of opinions up to his time. Cf. also K. Heussi, *Der Ursprung des Mönchtums* (Tübingen 1936) 1-10.

[25] *Ursprung des Mönchtums im nachkonstantinischen Zeitalter* (Gotha 1877).

[26] See below, the notes to the text, 6, 60, 244.

[27] Eichhorn, *op. cit.* 52, quoted by Robertson, *op. cit.* 191. See also Butler 1. 227 f.

[28] Cf. H. Delehaye, *Les légendes hagiographiques* (Subsidia hagiogr. 18 - 3rd ed. Brussels 1927) 68-70.

[29] Cf. v. Hertling, *op. cit.* 7-12.

[30] Cf. G. Bardy, *Saint Athanase* (Paris 1914) 48.

[31] Cf. P. Batiffol, *La paix constantinienne et la catholicisme* (3rd ed. Paris 1914) 445-7.

[32] *Hist. Laus.* 1 (2. 16 Butler).

[33] *Epist.* 127. 5. Cf. P. de Labriolle, in Fliche-Martin, *Histoire de l'Eglise* 3 (Paris 1947) 348 f.

[34] Cf. E. S. Duckett, *The Gateway to the Middle Ages* (New York 1938) 358 f.; M. L. W. Laistner, *Thought and Letters in Western Europe 500-900* (London 1921) 15.

[35] Cf. F. Blass, *Die attische Beredsamkeit* 2 (2nd ed. Leipzig 1892) 284-8.

[36] This forms the theme of List's monograph, *Das Antoniusleben des hl. Athanasius d. Grossen: eine literarhistorische Studie zu den Anfängen der byzantinischen Hagiographie* (Texte u. Forsch. ... byz.-neugr. Philol. 11, Athens 1930); cf. 62, his résumé.

[37] Cf. E. C. Marchand, *Xenophon, Scripta Minora* (Loeb Classical Library, London 1925) xviii-xix; Blass, *op. cit.* 2. 379-85.

[38] Cf. R. Reitzenstein, *Hellenistische Wundererzählungen* (Leipzig 1906) 55-59, for which see A. Puech, *Histoire de la littérature chrétienne* 3 (Paris 1930) 116; cf. also List, *op. cit.* 59-61.

[39] *Loc. cit.*

[40] List, *op. cit.* 61.

[41] From v. Hertling's final appraisal of Antony's stature—*op. cit.* 88. Here we may also quote the words of Cardinal Newman *(The Church of the Fathers*, in *Historical Sketches* 2 [New York-Bombay 1906] 111), previously cited by Butler 1. 228: 'His doctrine surely is pure and unimpeachable; and his temper is high and heavenly,— without cowardice, without gloom, without formality, and without

self-complacency. Superstition is abject and crouching, it is full of thoughts of guilt; it distrusts God, and dreads the powers of evil. Antony at least has nothing of this, being full of holy confidence, divine peace, cheerfulness, and valorousness. . . .'

[42] For this and the following, see the excellent observations by v. Hertling, op. cit. 47-56; also M. Viller–K. Rahner, Aszese und Mystik in der Väterzeit (Freiburg i. Br. 1938) 86 f.

[43] Cf. List, op. cit. 55-59.

[44] Cf. Viller-Rahner, loc. cit.

[45] Perhaps this was already in the Latin' version by Evagrius. Cf. H. Günter, Legendenstudien (Cologne 1906) 83 f.; H. Mertel, Des heiligen Athanasius Leben des heiligen Antonius (Bibl. d. Kirchenv. 31, Munich 1917) 1.

[46] St. Jerome, De viris ill. 125. An even earlier Latin translation, which is anonymous, was brought to light by A. Wilmart, 'Une version latine inédite de la Vie de saint Antoine,' Revue bénédictine 31 (1914) 163-73. It was edited by G. Garitte, Un témoin important du texte de la vie de saint Antoine par saint Athanase. La version latine inédite des Archives du Chapitre de Saint-Pierre à Rome (Etudes de philol., d'archéol. et d'hist. anc. 3, Brussels-Rome 1939).

[47] St. Augustine, Conf. 8. 6. 14: 'Then when I told him (Pontici-anus) that I spent a great deal of effort in the reading of Scripture, he began to tell me the story of Antony, the Egyptian monk whose name was famous among Thy servants, but up to then was un-known to us.' See ibid. 12. 29, and below, n. 13 to the text; also A. D. Nock, Conversion: the Old and the New in Religion from Alexander the Great to Augustine of Hippo (Oxford 1933) 265. For traces of St. Athanasius in the works of St. Augustine, see the study by B. Altaner, 'Augustinus und Athanasius. Eine quellenkritische Studie,' Rev. bénéd. 59 (1949) 82-90.

[48] See Altaner, art. cit. 87, who suggests that the other Latin version (cf. above, n. 46) was scarcely known in wider circles.

[49] Cf. M. Hélin, A History of Medieval Latin Literature (trans. by J. C. Snow, New York 1949) 118.

[50] For numerous illustrations of art depicting St. Antony and his life, see the book by C. Champion, Saint Antoine Ermite (L'art et les saints, Paris n. d.).

[51] Published by P. Bedjan, Acta martyrum et sanctorum 5 (Paris 1895) 1-121. Cf. also the recension made by the seventh-century monk Anan-Isho: The Book of Paradise, ed. by E. A. Budge

(London 1904) 1. 1-108 (Life of St. Anthony, trans.); 2. 1-93 (Syriac text). Cf. Bardenhewer 3. 67 f.

[52] A considerable number of sections have also been translated by Cardinal Newman and interspersed in his two chapters on Antony in *Historical Sketches 2: The Church of the Fathers* (New York-Bombay 1906) 94-126.

TEXT

[1] This heading, preserved in the Evagrian version, is probably the original one: *Athanasius episcopus ad peregrinos fratres.* The heading or title chosen by the Benedictine editors from several appearing in the Greek manuscripts reads: 'The life and conduct of our holy father Antony; composed and sent to the monks abroad by our holy father Athanasius, bishop of Alexandria.'

[2] Here there may be a reminiscence of Xenophon, *Mem.* 4. 1. 1: 'Even the remembrance of him (Socrates), though he is no longer with us, benefits not a little those who were wont to associate with him.'

[3] R. Reitzenstein, *Des Athanasius Werk über das Leben des Antonius* (Sitzungsb. d. Heidelb. Akad. d. Wiss. 8, 1914) 6 f., points to similar commonplaces in Lucian and Ps.-Lucian.

[4] Cf. 4 Kings 3. 11, where the same is said of Eliseus' attendance upon Elias. In my translation I follow the preponderance of the Greek MSS, reading παρὰ τοῦ ἀκολουθήσαντος ... καὶ ἐπιχέαντος, instead of παρ' αὐτοῦ ἀκολουθήσας ... καὶ ἐπιχέων, which makes Athanasius the companion and servant of Antony; in other words, according to the former reading Athanasius' principal source is a monk who lived with Antony a long time, while in the latter reading Athanasius is his own primary source. See v. Hertling's excellent defense of the former reading: *Antonius der Einsiedler* (Forsch. z. Gesch. d. innerkirchlichen Lebens 1, Innsbruck 1929) 7 n. 1.

[5] Sozomen, *Hist. Eccl.* 1. 13, says he was born at Coma in central Egypt. This may be a confusion arising from the fact that Athanasius repeatedly speaks of the home 'town' or 'village' (κώμη) of Antony; see v. Hertling, *op. cit.* 12 n. 1.

[6] Antony consistently despises the higher (Greek) learning: See below, § § 20, 33, 72.

[7] Cf. Gen. 25. 27.

[8] The word used for church: Κυριακόν = *Dominicum* = lit. 'that which is the Lord's' = 'the Lord's House.' Cf. the study of F. J. Dölger, 'Kirche als Name für den christlichen Kultbau. Sprach- und Kulturgeschichtliches zu den Bezeichnungen Κυριακόν, οἶκος κυριακός, *Dominicum, basilica,*' *Ant. u. Christ.* 6 (1941) 161-95.

⁹ Cf. Matt. 4. 20; 19. 27.

¹⁰ Cf. Acts 4. 35-7.

¹¹ Cf. Eph. 1. 18; Col. 1. 5.

¹² Matt. 19. 21.

¹³ Cf. St. Augustine's account, *Conf.* 8. 12. 29, of how he recalled this incident in the life of St. Antony and followed the voice admonishing him—*tolle, lege! tolle, lege!*—and found all darkness dispelled when he opened a volume containing St. Paul's epistles and read Rom. 13. 13 f.

¹⁴ The *arura* was 100 Egyptian cubits = 2756 (or 2737?) square meters. We see that also by American standards the farm was of goodly size, approximately 207 acres. See F. Hultsch, 'Arura,' RE 2 (1896) 1491.

¹⁵ Matt. 6. 34.

¹⁶ The *Apophthegmata patrum* 20 (MG 65. 81 C), relate: 'A brother who had renounced the world and distributed his possessions to the poor, but kept back a little for himself, came to the abbot Antony. When he had learned of this, the old man said: "If you wish to become a monk, go to yonder village, buy some meat, put it around your bare body, and then come here." When the brother had done this, the dogs and birds kept hacking away at his body. As he came before him, the old man inquired whether everything had been done as he had suggested. When the other pointed to his body cut to shreds, Antony said: "Those who have renounced the world, but wish to have money are thus attacked and massacred by the demons." '

¹⁷ Here we have the first occurrence of the word παρθενών in the Christian sense of, lit. 'a house or group of virgins.' At this early time (*ca.* 271) women religious generally still lived with their families, though meeting for common exercises; cf. M. Viller-K. Rahner, *Aszese und Mystik in der Väterzeit* (Freiburg i. Br. 1939) 49 f. McLaughlin translates 'sisterhood,' which also leaves it an open question whether in this passage παρθενών implies a place or home for religious—a convent. Later in the present biography, § 54, we are told that when Antony's sister had advanced in years in the practice of virginity, she became the superioress of a group of virgins. For further use of the term παρθενών by the Fathers, cf. Du Cange, *Gloss. ad script. med. et inf. graecitatis* (Lyons 1688) 1120 f. The word *nonna* = 'nun' appears to have been first used by St. Jerome, *Epist.* 22. 16.

[18] Gal. 4. 18.

[19] Regarding the manual labor of Antony and the other Egyptian monks, see A. T. Geoghegan, *The Attitude towards Labor in Early Christianity and Ancient Culture* (Stud. in Christ. Ant. 6, Washington 1945) 163-174.

[20] 2 Thess. 3. 10.

[21] Cf. Matt. 6. 6.

[22] On the necessity of continual prayer, see Tertullian, *De exhort. cast.* 10; Cyprian, *De dom. orat.* 34-6; Clement of Alexandria, *Strom.* 7. 7. 35. 1; Basil, *Epist.* 2 *(Ad Gregorium)*. 2; *Hom.* 4 *(In martyrem Iulittam)*. 3; Ambrose, *Comm. in Lucam* 7. 6. 88-90; John Chrysostom, *Comm. in Matt.* hom. 22. 5 f.; Augustine, *Enarr. in Ps.* 37. 14; etc. Of course, our Lord Himself had enjoined the same: Luke 18. 1; 21. 36. See also St. Paul's injunction, 1 Thess. 5. 17: *Pray without ceasing.*

[23] There is a reminiscence here of Luke 8.15—of those who, *hearing the word, keep it.* On the subject of Scripture reading by the ancient monks, see F. Bauer, 'Die Hl. Schrift bei den Mönchen des christlichen Altertums,' *Theol. u. Glaube* 17 (1925) 512-32. It was said of more than one monk that he had learned the Old and New Testaments by heart: cf. Palladius, *Hist. Laus.* 11 (2. 32 Butler): Ammonius; *ibid.* 18 (2.56 Butler): Marcus. Of the Pachomian monks at Tabennesi it is reported by Palladius, *ibid.* 32 (2. 96 Butler), that 'they repeat by heart the entire Scriptures.'

[24] See Palladius, *Hist. Laus.* 18 (2. 47 f. Butler), the account regarding Macarius of Alexandria.

[25] Antony here distills the sum and essence of all virtue—love of Christ and love of neighbor; cf. J. List, *Das Antoniusleben des hl. Athanasius d. Grossen* (Texte u. Forsch. z. byz.-neugr. Philol. 11, Athens 1925) 14. List, *ibid.* n. 4, remarks that in the present passage ten Christian virtues are mentioned as compared with the Aristotelian nine; for another list of ten Christian virtues, see below, § 17.

[26] Antony was eager to learn from all, but not, as v. Hertling appositely remarks (*op. cit.* 23), to best them by any ascetic 'records' of his own. His remarkable spiritual poise and his consideration for the feelings of others will be met with again and again in the pages that follow.

[27] Ὁ μισόκαλος καὶ φθονερός; similarly, below, § 9.

[28] Time and experience have made the Devil a past master of his

invidious craft. See St. Cyprian, *Ad Fortun.* 2: 'Adversarius vetus est et hostis antiquus, cum quo proelium gerimus. Sex millia annorum iam paene conplentur, ex quo hominem diabolus inpugnat. Omnia genera temptandi et artes atque insidias deiciendi usu ipso vetustatis edidicit,' etc. On the manifold wiles and untiring resourcefulness of the Evil One, cf. also Firmicus Maternus, *De.err. prof. rel.* 26. 4; Lactantius, *De op. Dei* 1. 7; Cyril of Jerusalem, *Cat.* 16. 15; Isidore of Pelusium, *Epist.* 3. 156; Cassian, *Coll.* 7. 9-24; Leo the Great, *Serm.* 16. 3; 89. 3; especially, too, St. Jerome's celebrated description of his experience with temptation while living a solitary life in the desert: *Epist.* 22 *(ad Eustochium).* 7; also *ibid.* 29 and *Epist.* 125 *(ad Rusticum).* 12. See below, nn. 40 and 89.

[29] Job 40. 11.

[30] Cf. Judith 16. 21; Eccli. 7. 19; Isa. 66. 24; Mark 9. 48 (Greek).

[31] The same sin as that to which he—the serpent—seduced Eve with the words (Gen. 3. 5.): *Eritis sicut dii,* 'You shall be as Gods.'

[32] This assumption of human flesh by the Savior is the topic of Athanasius' *De Incarnatione;* cf. especially chs. 8 and 9.

[33] 1 Cor. 15. 10.

[34] Ps. 111. 10 (the sinner); Mark 9. 17 (a demon).

[35] Black—*ater, niger,* μέλας—was not uncommonly used by the Romans and Greeks in a transferred moral sense to designate malice or wickedness (e.g., Cicero, *Pro Caecina* 10. 27; Horace, *Sat.* 1. 4. 81-5; Ovid, *Am.* 1. 13. 35-6; etc.) Early Christian usage is the same: cf. Hermas, *Past.* sim. 9. 1. 5 and 9. 19. 1; Origen, *In Cant. Cant.* hom 1. 6; Methodius of Philippi, *De sang.* 4. 2; etc. The transfer of the color black to the author of all evil and all inquity—the Devil—was very early and very common. He is called the Black One, ὁ Μέλας, by Ps.-Barnabas, 4. 10 and 20. 1 (cf. *ACW* 6. 41 and 63; also J. A. Kleist's note 36, p. 171 *ibid.*). Because Ethiopians and Egyptians were black or very dark of skin, the Devil was frequently designated by these national names: see, for instance, the *Passio SS. Perpetuae et Felicitatis* 10. 6, 8, 9, 14 *(Aegyptius); Acts of Peter* 22 (Ethiopian woman); *Acts of Xanthippe and Polyxena* 17 f. (Ethiopian king). On this very interesting subject, see F. J. Dölger, *Die Sonne der Gerechtigkeit und der Schwarze* (Liturgiegesch. Forsch. 2, Münster i. W. 1918) 49-83.

[36] Osee 4. 12.

[37] Ps. 117. 7.

[38] Rom. 8. 3 f.

[39] See 1 Peter 5. 8.

[40] Cf. Eph. 6. 11. For a graphic account of the persistence of the evil spirits in temptation, see the story of the monk Moses, who in his earlier years had been a profligate and a robber: Palladius, *Hist. Laus.* 19 (2. 60-62 Butler). Cf. above, n. 28, and below, n. 89.

[41] Cf. 1 Cor. 9. 27.

[42] 2 Cor. 12. 10.

[43] Phil. 3. 13.

[44] 3 Kings 17. 1. The word σήμερον = 'this day'; from which, according to Athanasius, Antony argued his point, is not found in the original of this verse.

[45] Courage is necessary when dealing with the Devil. See *Pastor Hermae*, mand. 7; mand. 12. 5 f.; Origen, *Cont. Cels.* 8. 36; Cyril of Jerusalem, *Cat.* 16. 19; Ambrose, *Exam.* 6. 49; Augustine, *Enarr. in Ps.* 61. 20.

[46] Cf. Rom. 8. 35.

[47] Ps. 26. 3.

[48] In the mythology of the ancients the servants and minions of the gods were often called dogs: thus the Griffins, Harpies, Furies, etc.; cf. Liddell-Scott-Jones, *A Greek-English Lexicon* 1. 1015.

[49] God stands by while Antony is tempted. See also Augustine, *Enarr. in Ps.* 34. 2 f.

[50] The promise was redeemed indeed—see below, § 93.

[51] Cf. Acts 8. 20, St. Peter's rejection of money offered by Simon Magus for the gift of imparting the Holy Spirit by the imposition of hands.

[52] This was the 'Outer Mountain' where St. Antony spent twenty years in retirement. It is at Pispir on the east bank of the Nile, about fifty miles south of Memphis. The Nitrian desert lay to the northwest across the Nile, directly south of Alexandria. To the south of Heracleopolis, on both sides of the Nile lay the 'great desert' of the Thebaid, the home of later Egyptian monasticism. See Butler 2.xcviii, for a map of this region in *ca.* 400 A.D.

[53] In *De Incarn.* 47, Athanasius states that in times past demons hid in various places and terrified people by playing upon their fancy. But that was changed by the appearance of the Divine Word—a mere Sign of the Cross breaks all such spells. Cf. *ibid.* 48; 53; also the present biography § § 23; 35; also Lactantius, *Epit. div. inst.* 46. Cyril of Jerusalem, *Cat.* 13. 3, states that the demons shake with fear when they see the Sign of the Cross made; etc.— Particularly interesting is the testimony by Julian the Apostate,

Epist. 79 (93 f. Bidez-Cumont), that the Christians protected themselves against demons by hissing at them and making the Sign of the Cross. See the very lucid passage in Cyril of Jerusalem, *Cat.* 16. 19; also below, n. 146. Cf. F. J. Dölger, 'Heidnische Begrüssung und christliche Verhöhnung der Heidentempel,' *Ant. u. Christ.* 3 (1932) 193-5.—On the terms σφραγίς = 'seal,' and σφραγίζειν = 'to seal,' 'to impress a seal,' as used here to signify the making of the Sign of the Cross, see F. J. Dölger, *Sphragis* (Stud. z. Gesch. u. Kult. d. Altert. 5. 3-4, Paderborn 1911) 171 f.

⁵⁴ Ps. 67. 2 f.

⁵⁵ *Ibid.* 117. 10.

⁵⁶ Rom. 8. 32.

⁵⁷ Not, of course, in our sense, but in the original sense—cells or other habitations of individual μοναχοί, *monachi*, 'monks,' or anchorites (from ἀναχωρεῖν = to 'withdraw,' 'retire'), who led a *lone* life, a life for themselves. These were loosely organized and under the spiritual guidance of Antony.

⁵⁸ A reminiscence of Heb. 3. 20 and 12. 23.

⁵⁹ The canal, here named after the city of Arsinoë, linked up the Nile and Lake Moeris (cf. Herodotus 2. 148). Arsinoë was the chief city of the *nomos* or district of the same name, the Fayûm of today. It lay approximately fifty miles west of Pispir. In the time of Herodotus, who visited it (cf. *ibid.*), it was called Crocodilopolis = 'city of crocodiles.' He speaks of a gigantic labyrinth built there, the lower chambers of which contained the sepulchres of kings and sacred crocodiles. See J. David, 'Aschmoun,' *Dict. d'hist. et de géogr. ecclés.* 4 (1930) 898 f.; R. Pietschmann, 'Arsinoë' no. 3, RE 2 (1896) 1277 f.

⁶⁰ This was in Coptic, the popular language of Egypt. It was the only language spoken by Antony: cf. Palladius, *Hist. Laus.* 21 (2. 69 Butler); also G. Bardy, *La question des langues dans l'Eglise ancienne* 1 (Paris 1948) 45 f. See below, n. 244.

⁶¹ Athanasius often speaks of this sufficiency: cf. *Cont. gent.* 1; *Epist. de Syn.* 6; *Epist. ad episc. Aegypti et Libyae* 4.

⁶² Ps. 89. 10.

⁶³ See 1 Cor. 15. 42.

⁶⁴ Rom. 8. 18.

⁶⁵ See St. Cyprian, *Ad Fortun.* 13; St. Ambrose, *De Iacob et vita beata* 1. 7. 28; Gregory of Nazianzus, *Orat.* 7. 17; John Chrysostom, *In Epist. ad Rom. hom.* 15. 10.

⁶⁶ See Eccle. 2. 18; 4. 8; 6. 2.

[67] St. Augustine, *Enarr. in Ps.* 38. 12, states that there is one way of taking earthly riches with us—by sending them ahead of us, in the hands of the poor.

[68] See Luke 17. 7-10.

[69] See Ezech. 33. 12 f.

[70] Rom. 8. 28.

[71] 1 Cor. 15. 31. See below, § 91 and n. 294.

[72] See Phil. 3. 13.

[73] See Gen. 19. 26.

[74] Luke 9. 62. Cf. Jerome, *Epist.* 3. 4, concerning the monk Bonosus; *Epist.* 71. 1, to Lucinius who had vowed continence in marriage; *Epist.* 118. 4, urging a rich widower to renounce his wealth completely.

[75] Luke 17. 21.

[76] Jos. 24. 23. 'Jesus' is the Greek form ('Ιησοῦς) of the Hebrew Yēshūa' = 'Joshua' or 'Josue.'

[77] Matt. 3. 3.

[78] James 1. 20.

[79] *Ibid.* 1. 15.

[80] Prov. 4. 23.

[81] Eph. 6. 12.

[82] It was commonly believed in Christian antiquity that the evil spirits used the air as their habitat and as the medium of their nefarious activity (cf. the present biography, 65). St. Paul writes to the Ephesians (2. 2) that in time past they had 'walked according to the course of this world, *according to the prince of the power of this air*'; cf. *ibid.* 6. 12. See Tatian, *Ad Graec.* 15. 8; Athenagoras, *Suppl.* 25. According to St. Augustine, *De civ. Dei* 8. 22, the demons, cast down from Heaven, were punished to live in the air as a dungeon; cf. *ibid.* 8. 15; Cassian, *Coll.* 8. 12; Peter Chrysologus, *Serm.* 9. Cf. E. Mangenot, 'Démon d'après les Pères,' DTC 4. 1 (1911) 339-84; J. Quasten, 'A Coptic Counterpart of a Vision in the Acts of Perpetua and Felicitas,' *Byzantion* 15 (1941) 1-9; also the observations by L. A. Arand in ACW 3. 123 n. 68.

[83] Origen, *Cont. Cels.* 7. 67, states that the subject of demonology is extensive and difficult.

[84] That is, the pagans.

[85] Φαντασίαις. The Greek religious myths, according to Justin, *Apol.* 1. 54, were inventions of the evil spirits. Christian baptism, of which the demons had heard through the Prophets, was aped

by the pagans in various religious purifications—again by demoniacal inspiration: *ibid.* 2. 62. Theophilus, *Ad Autol.* 2. 8, states that
the ancient Greek poets, beginning with Homer and Hesiod, were
inspired by phantoms instilled by deceitful spirits. The ancient
oracles were the work of the Devil and his demons: cf. *Mart.
Carpi, Papyli et Agathon.* 17 (11 Krüger); Origen, *Cont. Cels.*
7. 3-6, 35; 8. 62. Cf. also Lactantius, *Epit. inst. div.* 23.

[86] The ability to discern good and evil spirits *(discretio
spirituum)* is a gift of the Holy Spirit: see St. Paul, 1 Cor. 12. 7
and 10. See below, § 35 and n. 125.

[87] 2 Cor. 2. 11.

[88] See Ps. 139. 6.

[89] Of the two most severe trials to which Christians are subjected,
persecution and temptation—both the work of the Devil—the latter
is the more formidable and dangerous: cf. Leo the Great, *Serm.*
18. 1. Cf. above, nn. 28 and 40.

[90] Cf. above, § 13 and n. 53.

[91] Job 41. 10-13 (Sept.)—description of the leviathan.

[92] *Ibid.* 41. 19, 23 f. (Sept.), again said of the leviathan.

[93] Exod. 15. 9.

[94] Isa. 10. 14. For a similar application of this and the following
passage to Satan, see Athanasius, *Epist. ad episc. Aegypti et Libyae*
1. 2.

[95] See Job 40. 25, 26, 29 (Sept.), also with reference to the leviathan. The Syriac writer Isaac of Antioch in a metrical homily on
the Devil, *Hom.* 36. 20-30 (1. 454 f. Bedjan), describes him as a
roaring lion who frightens men, but cannot harm them because he
is muzzled.

[96] Cf. Luke 10. 19.

[97] Hab. 2. 15.

[98] Luke 4. 41.

[99] Cf. Jude 6.

[100] Ps. 49. 16.

[101] Ps. 38. 2.

[102] Ps. 37. 14 f.

[103] Cf. Athanasius, *De Incarn.* 47 f.; *Epist. ed episc. Aegypti et
Libyae* 1. 2; Justin, *Apol.* 2. 5; *Dial.* 45. 3; also Origen, *Cont. Cels.*
1. 31; Augustine, *Enchir.* 14. 50.

[104] John 8. 44.

[105] Cf. Eccli. 1. 25 (26).

[106] Cf. 4 Kings 19. 35.

[107] Cf. Job 1. 13 ff. and 2. 7.

[108] Cf. *ibid.* 1. 12.

[109] Matt. 8. 31. Cf. Gregory the Great, *Mor.* 2. 10. 16.

[110] Gen. 1. 26 f., 5. 1, 9. 6. The creation of man after God's image and likeness is a favorite topic of St. Athanasius: cf. *Cont. Gent.* 34; *De Incarn.* 3; *Cont. Ar.* orat. 2. 78-80; *Epist. fest.* 2. 2.

[111] Luke 10. 19.

[112] Tertullian, *Apol.* 22. 2, states that this quality—*subtilitas et tenuitas sua*—is of advantage to the demons in their assaults both upon the body and upon the soul of man.

[113] Origen, *Cont. Cels.* 4. 92 f., speaking of the practice of divination and augury, thinks that certain demons, because they are unencumbered by any corporeal substance, have in a measure the faculty of prognosticating future events. In order to seduce the human race away from the true God, they hide themselves in certain animals, for example, serpents and certain types of birds, and employ them to mislead the curious and credulous. See also Tertullian, *Apol.* 23; Minucius Felix, *Oct.* 26 f.; Cyprian, *Quod idola dii non sint* 7; Lactantius, *Div. inst.* 2. 17; Peter Chrysologus, *Serm.* 5; etc.

[114] Dan. 13. 42.

[115] The Nile, to the Egyptian that which makes Egypt, in much the same sense that to the Roman *Urbs* ('the City') was Rome. Interestingly enough, in the Hebrew Old Testament the Nile is never referred to by name, but termed simply, as here, 'the River.'

[116] The primitive, materialistic conception of the demons and their activity is quite apparent; cf. A. Robertson's pertinent note to H. Ellershaw's translation of the previous section, § 31. Regarding the present passage, we can well agree with the remarks by Viller-Rahner, *op. cit.* 86: 'That the Devil plays a quite too prominent role in these discourses will surprise no one who is familiar with the literature of the time. It is quite in point to take it good-humoredly when we are told that a demon, equipped as he is with a body lighter than man's, is capable of unusually swift locomotion and can foreannounce by several hours or days the floods of the Nile from having observed them in Ethiopia.' Regarding what some find to be 'ridiculous' or even 'buffoonish,' but others regard as good-naturedly and wholesomely 'humorous' in the ancient accounts of the desert monks versus the Devil, see the excellent observations by

Henri Brémond in his introduction to Jean Brémond, *Les pères du désert* (Paris 1927) 1.xxvii-xxx; also v. Hertling, *op. cit.* 56.

[117] 2 Kings 18. 24.

[118] That is, David; 'The man coming' — Achimaas, followed by Chusai; because actually there were two men approaching, Evagrius uses the plural—*venientes*.

[119] See also Athanasius, *De Incarn.* 47, where the various oracles are mentioned by name.

[120] On the soul's 'natural state' (cf. also above, § 20), see P. Resch, *La doctrine ascétique des premiers maîtres égyptiens du quatrième siècle* (Paris 1931) 5-13.

[121] See below, §§ 59, 62.

[122] 4 Kings 5. 26.

[123] *Ibid.* 6. 17.

[124] See Col. 2. 15.

[125] On distinguishing good and evil spirits, see above, § 22 and n. 86. Cf. Hermas, *Past.* mand. 5; Origen, *De princ.* 3. 2. 4 and 3. 3. 4. See Viller-Rahner, *op. cit.* 75; Resch, *op. cit.* 95-99.

[126] Matt. 12. 19 (see Isa. 42. 2).

[127] Ἀκύμαντοι, a highly poetic metaphor of the calm sea undisturbed by any waves—'waveless.'

[128] Luke 1. 13.

[129] Matt. 28. 5.

[130] Luke 2. 10. The most eminent example, of Gabriel reassuring the Blessed Virgin—*Fear not Mary* (Luke 1. 30)—is referred to two paragraphs further on.

[131] John 8. 56.

[132] Θεοτόκος, *Dei genetrix, deipara,* the celebrated title and term which had been employed for a long period to express Mary's motherhood, when in the first half of the fifth century it was attacked and defended in the Nestorian controversies and defined in the Council of Ephesus (431). According to the historian Sozomen, *Hist. Eccl.* 7. 32, the title had already been used by Origen; however, it is not found in the wreckage of the great Alexandrian's works. The first surviving record of the use of the title appears to be a letter by St. Alexander, bishop of Alexandria (313-28): cf. *Epist.* 1. 12 (= Rouët de Journel, *Enchiridion Patristicum,* 9th ed., no. 680). Alexander is followed by Eusebius of Caesarea and numerous other Fathers who employed the title as a common designation for the Blessed Mother. For the patristic evidence, see E.

Dublanchy, 'Marie, maternité divine: enseignement patristique' DTC 9. 2. (1927) 2349-55 (Athanasius: 2351 f.); also V. Schweitzer, 'Alter des Titels Θεοτόκος,' *Katholik* 3 ser. 17 (1903) 97-113.

133 Luke 1. 41.

134 See above, n. 130.

135 Matt. 4. 9.

136 *Ibid.* 4. 10. See Deut. 13. 4.

137 Σημεῖα, lit. 'signs,' a word often used in the New Testament (other words used: τέρατα and δυνάμεις—all three occur in Acts 2. 22 and 2 Cor. 12. 12) to designate Christ's miracles: Matt. 12. 38; 16. 1; Luke 23. 8; John 2. 11; 6. 26; etc.

138 Luke 10. 20.

139 Matt. 7. 22.

140 *Ibid.* 7. 23.

141 See Ps. 1. 6.

142 See 1 John 4. 1.

143 Ps. 19. 8.

144 Ps. 37. 14.

145 See above, n. 57.

146 For this passage, see F. J. Dölger, *Die Sonne der Gerechtigkeit und der Schwarze* 23 n. 1; also above, n. 35. Of numerous similar accounts of blowing one's breath or hissing at demons, the following quoted by Dölger (*Ant. u. Christ.* 3 [1932] 195) from H. Rosweyde, *Vitae Patrum* (2nd ed. Antwerp 1628) 379, may serve as an example. Pelagia, a penitent from Antioch, continued to be harassed by a demon even after she had been baptized. Bishop Nonnus advised her: 'Bless yourself with the Cross of Christ and renounce him.' This she did and the demon left her at once. But when during the night the demon began to molest her again, Pelagia rid herself of him in the following manner: 'Then Pelagia, the servant maid of God, blessed herself with the Sign of the Cross and blew a breath at the demon, saying: "May my God who has liberated me from your teeth and who has led me into His heavenly bridal chamber, resist you for me." And the Devil disappeared instantly.' See above, n. 53.

147 See Rom. 8. 35.

148 Luke 10. 18.

149 1 Cor. 4. 6.

150 On the Devil quoting Scripture, see Matt. 4. 6; Cassian, *Coll.* 1. 20 f.; *De Incarn.* 7. 16. See above, § 25.

151 See above, § 14.

152 Gregory the Great, *Mor.* 14. 13. 15, describes the Devil as an excellent psychologist who carefully surveys the temperament and inclinations of each prospective victim and chooses and sets his snares accordingly. Gregory also states pointedly (*ibid.* 2. 13. 22) that the Devil not only plots what to do, but when to do it.

153 See Rom. 12. 12.

154 Προσδοκῶντας, 'looking forward to,' 'expecting': an illustration of the belief often expressed in the Fathers, that the punishment with hell-fire had not yet begun, or at least had been interrupted, and, therefore, still lay ahead for Satan and his demons. Evidently this belief was based in good part on the account in the Apocalypse, especially Ch. 20, of Satan's war against the Church and of the Last Judgment (cf. 20. 9 f.: Satan and Antichrist are cast into the everlasting torment of fire and brimstone); on the account in the Apocalypse, see especially St. Augustine, *De civ. Dei* 20. 7-14. Justin Martyr, *Apol.* 1. 28, states that Christ foretold that Satan and his minions would be condemned to fire; in fact, according to the testimony of Irenaeus (*Adv. haer.* 5. 26. 3 Harvey), Justin held that prior to Christ's coming Satan abstained from blaspheming God because he was not yet aware of his condemnation. Tertullian, *Apol.* 27. 3, speaks of a delay in the punishment *(poenae mora)* of the demons; but adds that when they begin to serve their sentence, this will be all the more severe because of their part in fomenting the persecution of the Christians. St. Ambrose, *Comm. in Lucam* 6. 41, thinks that the demons who begged the Lord's permission to enter a herd of swine (Luke 8. 32), did so because they knew that at His coming glory they would be cast into the abysses of hell. Gregory of Nyssa, finally, appears to believe that after many centuries of purification the demons will be saved; see *Dial. de an. et ress.* 9. 2, and elsewhere. For further patristic evidence, cf. E. Mangenot, 'Démon d'après les Pères,' DTC 4. 1 (1911) 339-84.

155 See Matt. 25. 41.

156 See Jos. 5. 13 f.—Josue's vision of the warrior near Jericho.

157 See Dan. 13. 51-59—Daniel questioning the two wicked elders.

158 Antiquity's hatred and contempt for the class of tax-collectors was notorious. This was especially true of the little native officials serving as collectors for the entrepreneurs to whom the taxes were farmed out: cf. Cicero, *De off.* 1. 52. 150; Lucian, *Necyom.* 11;

Philo, *Spec. leg.* 2. 93; Gregory of Nazianzus, *Orat.* 19. 14 (where the apothegm: 'War is the father of taxes'!). For Egypt, see T. Frank, *An Economic History of Rome* (2nd ed. Baltimore 1927) 391-4. On this subject see also the informative article by H. C. Youtie, 'Publicans and Sinners,' *Mich. Alum. Quart. Rev.* 43 (1937) 650-62.

For a remarkable encomium of monastic Egypt—'this desert become fairer than any paradise'—see John Chrysostom, *In Matt. hom.* 8. 4 f. This Egypt, it is said, is proud of the lowly fisherman, and 'Everywhere they sing the praises of the *publican* and tentmaker'! On the other hand, we find St. Basil, the great protector of monks, making a most urbane plea (*Epist.* 284) with an assessor that he exempt them from taxation. He argues that if they are true monks, they own neither money nor bodies of their own: the former is spent in helping the needy, the latter is worn away by prayer and fasting. Cf. G. F. Reilly, *Imperium and Sacerdotium according to St. Basil the Great* (Stud. in Christ. Ant. 7, Washington 1945) 98 f.

[159] Num. 24. 5 f.

[160] See John 14. 2.

[161] Cf. the first sentence in Porphyry's *Life of Plotinus:* 'Plotinus, the philosopher who lived in our day, appeared to be ashamed of being in a body.'

[162] Luke 12. 22 and 29-31, with slight borrowings from the parallel passage in Matthew, 6. 31-33.

[163] When in the year 305 Diocletian and Maximianus abdicated as Emperors *(Augusti),* Constantius and Galerius succeeded them, and Severus and Maximin Daja (nephew of Galerius) were appointed Caesars. Maximin received the administration of Syria, Palestine, and Egypt. He was especially active in continuing the persecution of the Christians undertaken by Diocletian. Abetted by Galerius, this persecution lasted till the year 311. Celebrated victims of his cunning and savage cruelty included the martyrs Pamphilus of Caesarea, revered teacher of Eusebius, the bishop Methodius of Philippi (Olympus?), and Peter, bishop of Alexandria (see below, n. 169). On the persecution, see Eusebius, *De martyribus Palaestinae,* a supplement to bk. 8 of his *Ecclesiastical History.* See P. Allard, *La persécution de Dioclétien et la triomphe de l'Eglise* (2nd ed. Paris 1900) 166-205 and *passim;* A. Ehrhard, *Die Kirche der Märtyrer* (Munich 1932) 91 ff.

[164] On Antony's conduct in Alexandria and the historicity of the present episode, see v. Hertling, *op. cit.* 71 f.

[165] This recalls an incident told by Eusebius (*Hist. Eccl.* 5. 1. 49) concerning the conduct of a prominent physician, Alexander, during the persecution of the Christians in Gaul (A.D. 177/8). At a final hearing for such Christians as had already abjured their faith and who were to be set free, the court found that these abjured their former abjuration. Alexander had posted himself near the tribunal, where the mob saw him gesticulating to the prisoners, thus encouraging them to give witness for the faith. Cf. J. C. Plumpe, *Mater Ecclesia* (Stud. in Christ. Ant. 5, Washington 1943) 38.

[166] In other words, he changed the appearance of a monk to that of an Egyptian civilian. The Syriac version of Palladius' *Book of Paradise* (1. 57 Budge) adds that he 'made white the apparel with which he was clothed.' V. Hertling, *loc. cit.*, suggests that he may also have cut away his beard.

[167] Antony's own life of asceticism came to be looked upon as equivalent to martyrdom: cf. R. Reitzenstein, *Des Athanasius Werk über das Leben des Antonius* 19 n. 2. On the subject of equivalents for martyrdom and of the tendency of hagiographers to show that their unmartyred heroes had led lives as good and as heroic as the martyrs, see H. Delehaye, *Sanctus* (Stud. hagiogr. 17, Brussels 1927) 109-21: 'Du martyr au confesseur.'

[168] See Heb. 13. 3.

[169] Peter became bishop of Alexandria probably in the year 300 and was executed on November 25, 311. Eusebius, *Hist. Eccl.* 9. 6. 2, calls him 'an extraordinarily fine bishop, both for his life of virtue and for his competence in the Sacred Scriptures.' Of his writings only fragments remain. Cf. Bardenhewer 2. 239-470; G. Fritz, 'Pierre d'Alexandrie,' DTC 12. 1 (1935) 1802-4.

[170] Jerome, *Vita S. Hilar.* 4, relates that Antony dismissed the boy monk Hilarion with the gift of such a garment of skins.

[171] Porphyry, *Vita Plot.* 2, relates the same of Plotinus. Instances of the practice as recounted by Palladius, *Hist. Laus.* are: 1 (2. 15 Butler), the Alexandrian priest Isidore; 38 (2. 122 Butler), the Iberian deacon Evagrius. The Palestinian solitary, Hilarion, never washed the sackcloth he wore—so Jerome, *Vita S. Hilar.* 10. See also Serapion of Thmuis, *Ep. ad mon.* 2; Gerontius, *Vita S. Melaniae iun.* 2; Diadochus, *Cap. cent. de perf. spir.* 50 f. The

shunning of the bath was, of course, bound up with the motive of
performing penance; but at the basis of this form of asceticism lay
also a profound abhorrence of the notorious licentiousness prevalent
in the pagan public baths: cf. Clement of Alexandria, *Paed.* 3. 5;
John Chrysostom, *In Matt.* hom. 7. 6 f.; etc. On ancient asceticism
and bathing, see J. Zellinger, *Bad und Bäder in der altchristlichen
Kirche* (Munich 1928) 47-92.

[172] Luke 11. 9.

[173] This reminds us of the ancient practice known as *incubation.*
Persons desirous of receiving a vision or relief from sickness slept
within the precincts of a temple. The practice, for which various
observances and rites (fasting, sleeping on certain pelts, etc.) were
prescribed, was particularly prevalent in the temples of Asclepius
(god of health), and later spread to the shrines of Isis and Serapis.
See J. Pley, 'Inkubation,' RE 9 (1916) 1256-62; R. Herzog, *Die
Wunderheilungen von Epidaurus* (Philologus Supplementb. 22. 3,
Leipzig 1931) 139-160. Cf. J. Quasten, *Theol. Rev.* 30 (1931)
540 f.; A. Chaudre, 'Inkubation,' LTK 5 (1933) 406 f.

[174] See 2 Cor. 12. 4.

[175] Tὰ Βουκόλια, a swampy district in the Nile delta inhabited by
herdsmen; cf. K. Sethe, 'βουκόλοι,' RE 3 (1898) 1013. Here the
'voice' intimates that Antony had reflected not only on going in a
southerly direction, but also on heading to the north.

[176] Originally a tribe in Arabia, probably mentioned already by
Pliny, *Nat. hist.* 6. 32. 157 (as *Araceni*). Saracens later became
synonymous with Arabs and in the time of the Crusades the name
was used for Moslems.

[177] Mount Colzim, lying in the open desert on the South Qalala
Plateau, approximately 100 miles south-east of Cairo, 75 miles east
of the Nile, and 20 miles west of the Red Sea. The mountain, with
the ancient Monastery of St. Antony, is still called Dêr Mar
Antonios. See P. F. Anson, *The Quest of Solitude* (London 1932)
15 f. Antiquity has preserved for us a detailed description of the
locality, specifically of the 'Inner Mountain,' in St. Jerome's *Vita
S. Hilarionis* (30 f.). See also v. Hertling, *op. cit.* 35-43. Regarding
the remark that Antony 'fell in love with the place,' the same is
reported by St. Jerome with respect to Paul of Thebes when he had
found his mountain cave: *Vita S. Pauli* 6.

[178] One of the stock incidents of hagiography. See Jerome, *Vita
S. Hilar.* 31, a replica of the present narrative, though Antony is

there described as thrashing the wild ass he had caught. The *Acta SS* for August, VI (1868) 72. 36, tells of a great number of wild boars which are abjured by St. Caesarius of Arles to leave the neighborhood of his monastery. On animal stories as a characteristic of the records of the Egyptian monks, cf. W. H. Mackean, *Christian Monasticism in Egypt to the Close of the Fourth Century* (London 1920) 137.

[179] The terminology of the ancient athletic events is used metaphorically by St. Paul (Eph. 6. 12; 1 Cor. 2. 24; Phil. 3. 14; 2 Tim. 4. 7; etc.) and the early Christian writers to portray the life of effort and trial which a Christian must take upon himself if he wishes to get to Heaven. See especially St. Basil's panegyrics on the martyrs, *passim*. On the saints as God's athletes, see H. Delehaye, *Les passions des martyres et les genres littéraires* (Brussels 1921) 211 f. See the articles 'ἀγών' and 'ἀθλητής' in TWNT 1 (1933); also F. J. Dölger, 'Der Kampf mit dem Aegypter in der Perpetua-Vision,' *Ant. u. Christ.* 3 (1932) 177-88; E. L. Hummel, *The Concept of Martyrdom according to St. Cyprian of Carthage* (Stud. in Christ. Ant. 9, Washington 1946) 79-87.

[180] See Eph. 6. 12.

[181] Ps. 124. 1.

[182] See Job 5. 23.

[183] See Ps. 34. 16.

[184] Χριστοῦ δοῦλος, as St. Paul frequently calls himself: Rom. 1. 1; Phil. 1. 1; Gal. 1. 10.

[185] That is, the word (Word) 'Christ.'

[186] One can scarcely be impressed by the erudition of K. Heussi, *Der Ursprung des Mönchtums* (Tübingen 1936) 98, when he remarks that 'here there is an echo of an old *legendary motif*' (italics mine) and refers to the Old Testament miracle of the rock struck by Moses.

[187] See Rom. 1. 12.

[188] See Prov. 24. 15 (Sept.).

[189] Eph. 4. 26.

[190] 2 Cor. 13. 5.

[191] Daily examination of conscience, not entirely unknown to the pagan mind (see Seneca, *De ira* 3. 36. 1-3; *Epist.* 83. 2), was often recommended by the Fathers: see St. Basil, *Serm. ascet.* 1. 5; St. John Chrysostom, *In Matt.* hom. 42. 3 f.; *In Epist. ad Heb.* 9. 5; St. John Climacus, *Scala parad.* 4. The examination is prominently

mentioned in the monastic rules. Cf. G. Sepiéter, *L'examen de conscience* (2nd ed. Lille 1932).

[192] See 1 Cor. 4. 5; Rom. 2. 16.

[193] Gal. 6. 2.

[194] 1 Cor. 9. 27.

[195] A Roman name, as is the name of the town from which Fronto is said to have come. Though there were at least two towns in ancient Italy that went by the name Palatium, the further, normal meaning of the word as 'palace,' 'court,' suggests that the man, otherwise unknown, was a Roman official or employee connected with the palace of the Roman prefect in Alexandria.

[196] It seems quite impossible to unscramble this combination of town and province. There were several towns in Egypt called Busiris (cf. F. Hiller v. Gaertringen, 'Busiris,' RE 3. 1 [1897] 1073-7); and besides the province so named in northern Africa, there were in antiquity several groups of towns or communities that went by the name Tripolis (cf. 'Tripolis' RE 2. R., 7. 1 [1939] 202-10: Nos. 8 [E. Kirsten], 9 and 10 [F. Bölte]); but a Busiris in Tripoli(s) appears to be simply bad geography on the part of Athanasius.

[197] See Matt. 9. 20.

[198] The name Paphnutius was most common in Egypt of the fourth century. There are at least a half-dozen bishops and monks by that name, and sometimes it is quite impossible to establish which Paphnutius is meant in certain ancient data; see Butler 2. 224; H. I. Bell, *Jews and Christians in Egypt* (London 1924) 101. In the present instance, however, the addition of the title 'confessor' makes it quite certain that the bishop of the Upper Thebaid who was tortured under Maximian (so Evagrius and Rufinus—Sozomen reads Maximin) is referred to. He had lost his right eye and his left knee was maimed. He was highly honored at the great Council of Nicaea and took a prominent part in it. Cf. Socrates, *Hist. Eccl.* 1. 8 and 11; Sozomen, *Hist. Eccl.* 1. 4; Theodoret, *Hist. Eccl.* 1. 6. See Acta SS Sept. III (1868) 778-87; J. Hefele-H. Leclercq, *Histoire des conciles* 1. 1 (Paris 1907) 429 f., and 620-4; M. M. Hassett, 'Paphnutius,' *Cath. Encycl.* 11 (1911) 457.

[199] On 'second sight' and similar endowments of the desert solitaries, cf. E. W. Watson, 'Palladius and Egyptian Monasticism,' *Church Quart. Rev.* 64 (1907) 123 f.

[200] The story of Amoun (also Amon, Ammon, originally the name

of an Egyptian deity) is told by Palladius, *Hist. Laus.* 8 (2. 26-29 Butler). He was an orphan of a prominent family, and married at the insistence of his uncle. He and his wife lived a life of virginity for eighteen years, whereupon, at her suggestion, he left her (A.D. 320-330) to become a monk in the Nitrian desert west of the Nile delta. He lived there for twenty years till his death, having visited his wife twice annually. By the end of the fourth century the desert of Nitria held five thousand disciples of Amoun. The incidents related by Athanasius in the present section are also adverted to by Palladius. See also *Hist. monach. in Aegypto* 29. 1 (90 Preuschen); Socrates, *Hist. Eccl.* 4. 23; Sozomen, *Hist. Eccl.* 1. 14 and 6. 28; cf. also Acta SS Oct. II (1866) 413-22; Mackean, *op. cit.* 81 f.; J. P. Kirsch, 'Ammon,' LTK 1 (1930) 367.

[201] The Venerable Bede relates a similar incident regarding St. Cuthbert: *Vita Cuthberti* 4.

[202] Palladius, *Hist. Laus.* 8 (28 f. Butler), and Sozomen, *Hist. Eccl.* 1. 14, state that this was a canal branching out from the Nile—probably at Lycopolis in Upper Egypt.

[203] A favorite name with the desert monks, and the identity of Amoun's companion escapes detection.

[204] Matt. 14. 29.

[205] On the ancient metaphor of death as a sleep and the note of cheer and hope attaching to it for the early Christians (note also κοιμητήριον = 'cemetery,' lit. 'a sleeping place'), cf. A. C. Rush, *Death and Burial in Christian Antiquity* (Stud. in Christ. Ant. 1, Washington 1941) 1-22: 'Death as a Sleep.'—For further 'same day and hour' incidents, see Palladius, *Hist. Laus.* 4 (2. 20 f. Butler): Didymus the Blind regarding the death of Julian the Apostate; Theodoret, *Hist. Eccl.* 3. 19: the monk Julianus regarding the death of the same.

[206] Perhaps the high official who assisted Athanasius in unmasking some of the machinations of the Eusebians and Meletians at the Synod of Tyre in the year 335; see Hefele-Leclercq, *Histoire des conciles* 1. 2 (1907) 656-66. The title given to Archelaus, κόμης, transliterated from the Latin *comes* (hence the English 'count'), was an imperial designation for officials of various ranks. The statement by Rufinus, *Hist. Eccl.* 1. 16, that the Archelaus mentioned was *comes Orientis*, the governor of the Orient, is accepted by R. Reitzenstein, 'Archelaos' no. 31, RE 2. 1 (1895) 452 f., but seriously doubted by Bell, *op. cit.* 67.

124 NOTES

[207] Polycratia as a woman's name occurs rather frequently in ancient Greek inscriptions (cf. W. Pape—G. F. Benseler, *Wörterbuch der griechischen Eigennamen* [2nd ed. Braunschweig 1884] *s.v.*); but apparently it is not found with the ancient hagiographers It is not clear either which Laodicea is meant: there were a numbe of cities by that name, the most prominent of which lay in Syri and Phrygia.

[208] Χριστοφόρος ('Christopher' = 'Christ-bearer') had been in use as a title for the good Christian since Ignatius of Antioch (cf. *Ad Ephes.* 92, and J. A. Kleist in ACW 1 [1946] 64 and 122 with n. 27). The designation probably has its roots in St. Paul, Gal. 3. 27: 'As many of you as have been baptized in Christ, have put on Christ.' During the persecutions it became a favorite title for the martyrs: Christ resides in them, their courage and ability to suffer are from Him, it is He who fights and is victorious in them. In the fourth century, with the end of the persecutions and the rise of monasticism, the title was given especially to men and women ascetics (many parallels between martyrdom and asceticism were seen). Cf. the most interesting papyrus letter reproduced and translated by Bell, *op. cit.* 108 f. Here a certain Valeria, suffering from a serious case of asthma, addresses herself to a monk Paphnutius, calling him Χριστοφόρος. She states: 'I trust by your prayers to obtain healing, for by ascetics and devotees revelations are manifested.' See the excellent study by F. J. Dölger, 'Christophoros als Ehrentitel für Martyrer und Heilige im christlichen Altertum,' *Ant. u. Christ.* 4 (1933) 73-80.

[209] Here called ἐνεργούμενος. In ancient Christian times the *energumeni* were persons subject to demoniacal disturbances. Insanity and epilepsy were also ascribed to such influence. In the fourth century the *energumeni* constituted a special class of the Church's subjects, standing between the catechumens and the penitents; a very detailed ritual of exorcism was also developed. See J. Sauer, 'Energumenen,' LTK 3 (1931) 671 f.; H. Leclercq, 'Exorcisme, Exorciste' DACL 5. 1 (1922) 964-78; for their place in the liturgy, J. Quasten, *Monumenta eucharistica et liturgica vetustissima* (Bonn 1935) Index *s.v.*

[210] See Luke 11. 24.

[211] Dividing the day into twelve hours, of shorter or longer duration according to the season of the year, this appears to have been between one and three o'clock in the afternoon.

[212] On ecstasy (ἔκστασις, in the ancient concept = the soul 'stepping out' of the body temporarily), see Tertullian, *De anima* 45. 3, and the notes by J. H. Waszink, *Quinti Septimi Florentis Tertulliani De Anima* (Amsterdam 1947) 484 f.; also Augustine, *Serm.* 12. 4. 4, and the *Apophthegmata Patrum: De Abb. Silvano* (MG 65. 408C). Cf. F. Pfister, 'Ekstasis,' in the *Festschrift* for F. J. Dölger: *Pisciculi. Studien zur Religion und Kultur des Altertums* (Münster i. W. 1939) 178-91.

[213] Cf. A. C. Rush, *op. cit.* 32-43.

[214] Eph. 2. 2.

[215] *Ibid.* 6. 13.

[216] Titus 2. 8.

[217] 2 Cor. 12. 2.

[218] *Ibid.* 12. 2.

[219] See Isa. 54. 13; John 6. 45; 1 Thess. 4. 9.

[220] Because he had the gift of discerning the promptings of good and evil spirits—see above, nn. 86 and 125. Cf. above, § 49: Antony was 'used to hearing such calls often.'

[221] See Dan. 9. 23.

[222] See Luke 24. 45.

[223] The ancient concept of the soul as something spiritual, or as something immaterial or nearly immaterial, is perhaps best illustrated by the effort, both pagan and Christian, to represent it in art, on tombstones and other monuments. Attempts to picture the soul as a phantom (εἴδωλον), representations of it as a minute being—frequently with wings—and similar portrayals document this concept of the soul's nature and its flight from the body at the moment of death. See the materials, with illustrations, offered in the article by H. Leclercq: 'Ame,' DACL 1. 1 (1924) 1470-554 (particularly interesting the monument, col. 1481, of a departed Christian infant, showing her fitted with Icarian wings!). The conviction of the ancients, both pagan and Christian, that when death occurs, the soul is beset by grave dangers, was symbolized—in literature (e.g. Origen, *In Luc.* hom. 23; Macarius, *Hom.* 22 and 43; Cyril of Alex., *De exitu an.* hom. 14; etc.) and art—by dragons, lions, and other demoniacal representations: cf. especially A. C. Rush, *op. cit.* 23-43; also J. Quasten, 'Der Gute Hirte in frühchristlicher Totenliturgie und Grabeskunst,' in *Miscellanea Giovanni Mercati* 1 (Studi e testi 121, Vatican City 1946) 373-406: Christ in ancient Christian art is shown as the *psychopompos*, the

Guide and Protector of souls on their dangerous passage into eternity.

224 Τὸν κανόνα τῆς 'Εκκλησίας, that is, the validly and officially appointed clergy of varying (hierarchic) rank in the performance of their ministry. For the history of the important term κανών (κανονικός, canon, canonicus) since its use in the New Testament (2 Cor. 10. 13, 15, 16; Gal. 6. 16) and during the first centuries of the Church (beginning with Clement of Rome 7. 2), see H. W. Beyer, TWNT 3 (1938) s.v., 600-606; F. Cabrol, 'Canon romain,' DACL 2. 2 (1925) 1847 f. ('le mot canon'); also H. Oppel, Κανών. Zur Bedeutungsgeschichte des Wortes und seiner lateinischen Entsprechungen, regula - norma (Leipzig 1937); J. P. Christopher, ACW 2. 109 n. 89.

225 The word (κλῆρος, κληρικός, clerus, clericus) appears to occur first in Tertullian (De monog. 12) and Origen (In Jer. hom. 11. 3). Cf. B. Dolhagaray, 'Clercs,' DTC 3. 1 (1908) 225-35.

226 It should be remembered that only a very few monks were also priests or in sacred orders at all (see Viller-Rahner, op. cit. 198 f.). The life of independence they led in the desert and their life of asceticism as compared with the life of the clergy serving the needs of the people in the world could easily prompt them to think little of the 'seculars.' Elsewhere, Epist. ad Dracont. 9, Athanasius suggests that monks must not depreciate the secular clergy. Among the canons issued by a synod held against the Priscillianists at Saragossa, Spain, in or about 380, no. 6 prescribes that a cleric who out of pride turns monk, supposing this to be a better observance of the law, shall be excommunicated (Hefele-Leclercq, Histoire des conciles 1. 2 [1907] 987).

227 Antony, in other words, possessed in a very high degree Christian ἀπάθεια—perfect self-control, freedom from passion—the ideal of every true monk and ascetic striving for perfection. Christ, who was free from every emotional weakness and fault— ἀπαθὴς Χριστός— is his model (see Athanasius, De Incarn. 54). He is farthest from Stoic apathy, he loves God intensely, he is not indifferent toward his fellow man but his fellow man's happiness is his joy; as Evagrius Ponticus, De orat. 122, states: 'Blessed the monk who joyfully regards the welfare and progress of all men as his own.' Cf. Viller-Rahner, op. cit. 107 f. The concept of Christian ἀπάθεια was first developed by Clement of Alexandria (e.g. Paed. 1. 2; Strom. 6. 9) and his pupil Origen (e.g. In Jerem. 5. 8 f.). On Christian ἀπάθεια

among the Fathers, especially, too, the ancient writers on asceticism
—Evagrius, Palladius, John Climacus, etc.—see J. Stiglmayr, *Sach-
liches und Sprachliches bei Makarius* (Innsbruck 1912) 66 ff.; also
P. de Labriolle, in Fliche-Martin, *Histoire de l'Eglise* 3 (1936)
336-8.

228 Prov. 15. 13.

229 Gen. 31. 5.

230 See 1 Kings 16. 12.

231 Named after Meletius, bishop of Lycopolis in Egypt (*ca.* 325)
and not to be confused with the Antiochene bishop and schism a
half century later. The earlier Meletian schism seems to have
originated from Meletius' disagreement with Peter, bishop of Alexandria, over the treatment of the lapsed during the Decian persecution, and also from Meletius' arrogation of the right to ordain
priests and bishops to replace the imprisoned clergy. The Council
of Nicaea took measures against him. His followers now went into
the camp of the Arians and became especially prominent in the
bitter struggles against our present reporter on them—St. Athanasius. This is vividly documented in the records of the Synod of
Tyre in 335 (see above, n. 206). Cf. E. Amann, 'Mélèce de Lycopolis,' DTC 10. 1 (1928) 531-6.

232 An old Gnostic heresy named after its founder Mani whose
approximate dates are 216 and 275. A conglomerate of Zoroastrian,
Hellenistic, and Christian elements, Manichaeism spread to practically all Christianized countries and survived in certain parts of
Asia into the Middle Ages. Perhaps its most celebrated disciple was
the young Augustine of Tagaste. See G. Bardy, 'Manichéisme,'
DTC 9. 2 (1927) 1841-95.

233 Εὐσέβεια (εὐσεβής), used here, and ἀσέβεια (ἀσεβής) found below, lit. meaning 'piety' and 'impiety,' regularly stand for 'orthodoxy' and 'heterodoxy'; cf. Card. Newman's remarks, *Select Treatises*, etc.—see the following note—2 (9th impression London 1903)
410 f.

234 The great heresy of the fourth century, named after Arius,
who was born in Libya in the second half of the third century, was
ordained priest by bishop Achilles of Alexandria, and died suddenly
in 336. The history of this Christological heresy, which denied
both the divinity and the humanity of Christ, also contains the life
story of St. Athanasius, whose bitter struggles of more than four
decades with the heresy date from the time he was deacon at

Alexandria; and still one of the best for the study of both, Arianism
and Athanasius, is Cardinal Newman in his two works: *The Arians
of the Fourth Century*, first published in 1833, and *Select Treatises of St. Athanasius in Controversy with the Arians*, which first
appeared in 1842 and 1844 as a translation with notes and consti-
tuting volumes 8 and 19 of the series *A Library of Fathers of the
Holy Catholic Church*, and in 1881 was published apart, again in
two volumes, the first of which contained a freer version of the
text, and the second an appendix consisting of nearly five hundred
pages of articles of varying length on theological subjects and terms.
For more recent treatment of the heresy, cf. A. Stohr, 'Arianismus,'
LTK 1 (1930) 635-41; G. Bardy, in Fliche-Martin, *Histoire de
l'Eglise* 3 (Paris 1936) 69 ff.

235 Athanasius has Δεισιδαιμονία, a name used not only by him,
but by the emperor Constantine and the general Church for the
followers of Arius. While it most obviously designates 'the followers of the madness of Arius,' 'the Arius-crazy,' the title also implies the fanaticism with which the heresy spread and maintained
itself; for this and further touches of meaning, see the discussion
and wealth of material in Card. Newman's note, *Select Treatises*
(9th impression) 2. 377-9.

236 There is very good authority for believing that this brief visit
to Alexandria was made shortly before July 27, 337 or 338; cf. v.
Hertling, *op. cit.* 73 n. 1. Antony's activity there against the Arians
is described briefly by Theodoret, *Hist. Eccl.* 4. 27.

237 'Ην ποτε, ὅτε οὐκ ἦν (see, too, above— ἐξ οὐκ ὄντων ἐστίν = 'He
has His existence from non-existence'), the celebrated formula of
Arius as recorded in the encyclical letter of Bishop Alexander of
Alexandria and preserved by Socrates, *Hist. Eccl.* 1. 6; cf. the
heresiarch's own letter to Eusebius of Nicomedia, preserved by
Theodoret, *Hist. Eccl.* 1. 5. 3.

238 2 Cor. 6. 14.

239 Rom. 1. 25.

240 Χριστομάχος, like θεομάχος = 'fighting against God' (cf. Acts
5. 39, also 23. 9). Both terms are used very frequently by Athanasius and others in reference to heretics; cf. Newman, *Select Treatises* 2. 415.

241 Ἑλληνες, Greeks—see above, n. 84.

242 Obviously Athanasius was in Alexandria on this occasion.

243 Socrates, *Hist. Eccl.* 4. 25, relates another incident, apparently

happening on Antony's way to Alexandria: 'It is said that earlier
already, in the time of Valens, Antony had met this Didymus when
he went down to Alexandria from the desert because of the Arians;
and that when he perceived the intelligence of the man, he said
to him: "Didymus, you must not let the loss of your physical eyes
grieve you. After all, the eyes that you lack are such as also flies
and gnats see with. You should rather rejoice that you have eyes
with which angels see, eyes which serve the contemplation of God
Himself and the reception of His light." '

The desert monk and scholar Didymus had lost his sight at the
age of four (Palladius, *Hist. Laus.* 4 [2. 19 Butler]). Socrates, incidentally, must have erred in his chronology: this last journey of
Antony to Alexandria very probably was made in 337 or 338 (see
above, n. 236); Valens, born about 328, was appointed emperor of
the East in 364; and at this latter date Antony was already dead,
having passed away probably in 356 or 357. Sozomen, *Hist. Eccl.*
3. 15, who takes this story from Socrates, evidently noticed Socrates'
error and dropped the reference to Valens.

²⁴⁴ Γράμματα μὴ μαθών, lit. 'not having learned letters'—see also
the following § 73: ὅτι μὴ μεμάθηκε γράμματα . As v. Hertling
rightly remarks (see his long note, *op. cit.* 14 f.), this does not
necessarily mean that he did not know how to read or write, but
only that he had not received the rhetorical and humanistic training usual with sons of parents as comfortably situated as were
Antony's. Yet, as Athanasius states at the beginning of this biography, Antony 'did not take to schooling,' and the context there
may well be taken to indicate that he was rather successful in his
desire to stay at home. Moreover, antiquity took the statement
literally that he was unlettered; so, for example, Augustine in the
prologue to the *De doctrina Christiana*. Regarding the fact that
Athanasius (§ 81 below) and Jerome (*Vita S. Hilar.* 24) report that
Antony exchanged letters with Constantine and other men in high
position and corresponded with various monks, this does not prove
that he could read and write: as he used interpreters in dealing
with Greeks, so a fellow monk could assist him as reader and
amanuensis. Cf. Bardenhewer 3. 80 f.; again, regarding the letters
handed down under Antony's name, v. Hertling, *op. cit.* 56-70.

²⁴⁵ Cassian, *Inst.* 5. 33 f., quotes the abbot Theodore, a master of
Scripture interpretation, as saying that one who has a pure heart
and, as a result, a clear mind, has all that is required for the under-

standing of the mysteries of Holy Scripture and has no need of laboring over commentaries.

[246] Socrates, *Hist. Eccl.* 4. 23, relates: 'To the good Antony there came a philosopher of the day and said: "Father, how do you hold up deprived as you are of the solace of books?" Antony said: "My book, philosopher, is nature, and thus I can read God's language at will." '

[247] Lit. 'with divine salt': cf. Col. 4. 6 and Mark 9. 49.

[248] Attracted, no doubt, by the account of the other groups just mentioned.

[249] Cf. Athanasius, *De Incarn.* 53, where he eloquently describes the routing of the gods by the Cross and the acceptance of the crucified Savior by the pagans ('Greeks') who once jeered Him; cf. *ibid.* 1; *Cont. Ar.* 1. 43; Leo the Great, *Serm.* 70. 3; etc. To be God and to be crucified was a paradox which from the beginning was a stumbling block to the Jews and spelled sheer folly to the pagans (see 1 Cor. 1. 23). See Tertullian's defense (*Apol.* 16; *Ad nat.* 1. 12) against the notorious charge that Christians adore the Cross and an ass's head; so, too, Minucius Felix, *Oct.* 29. In this connection it is pointed out that the 'infamy of the Cross' must be understood from the fact that in the world empire of the Romans crucifixion was the most disgraceful form of capital punishment, one reserved for slaves, pirates, and thieves. But it is often overlooked that this penalty remained in force well into the fourth century, coexistent, therefore, with the rise and full development of Christianity from that Cross. The position of Christians explaining and defending their allegiance to it was not easy, and non-Christians could be in very good faith if they could not see rhyme or reason in such allegiance. See the very instructive introductory remarks by H. Leclercq in his article, 'Croix et Crucifix,' DACL 3. 2 (1914) 3045-8.

[250] See 2 Peter 1. 4.

[251] Here two well-known elements of ancient psychology are adverted to, the pre-existence and the transmigration (metempsychosis) of the soul. Within the Greek sphere of thought and religion this teaching is found particularly in Orphism, Pythagoras, Plato, the Gnostics, and Neo-Platonism. For the present passage Neo-Platonism as developed by Plotinus, a native of Egypt and pupil of Ammonius Saccas in Alexandria, seems to offer the material for Antony's (or Athanasius') polemic; see Plotinus, *Enn.* 1. 1. 12;

3. 4. 2, 5; 4. 3. 15; etc. Cf. R. Hedde, 'Métempsychose,' DTC 10. 2 (1929) 1574-95; P. O. Kristeller, *Der Begriff der Seele in der Ethik des Plotin* (Heidelb. Abh. z. Philos. u. ihrer Gesch. 19, Tübingen 1929).

[252] The word παρουσία is used here: 'presence,' 'arrival,' 'coming,'—first employed in a technical sense in the profane sphere to designate the official visit of a ruler or other high personage. It is found frequently in the New Testament, notably in the Epistles of St. Paul (e.g. 1 Cor. 15. 23; 1 Thess. 2. 19; 2 Thess. 2. 1), and is there employed as a standing term for the second coming of Christ at the Last Judgment. Early in the second century the term began to be used to refer also to the first coming of Christ in His Incarnation and Redemption (see Ignatius of Antioch, *Philad.* 9. 2; Justin Martyr, *Apol.* 1. 52. 3; etc.); quite certainly this second sense is intended in the present passage. Cf. J. Chaine, 'Parousie,' DTC 11. 2 (1932) 2043-54; J.-B. Colon, 'Paul (Saint): la parousie,' *ibid.* 2388-99; P. Gächter, 'Parusie,' LTK 7 (1935) 990-2.

[253] The third of Plotinus' Triad of Divine Principles, the 'World-Soul' ('All-Soul,' 'Soul of the All,' 'Cosmic Soul')–Ψυχή –from which the individual souls diverge or emanate. See W. R. Inge, *The Philosophy of Plotinus* (3rd ed. London 1929) 1. 200-64; E. Bréhier, *La philosophie de Plotin* (Paris 1928) 47-79; K. Prächter, *Die Philosophie des Altertums*, in F. Ueberweg, *Grundriss der Geschichte der Philosophie* 1 (Berlin 1926) 603 f.

[254] That is, the Incarnation of the Son of God, the coming of Christ, just referred to.

[255] Also rendered the 'Intelligence' or 'Spirit'—the Νοῦς –the second of Plotinus' Triad of Divine Principles; see especially *Enn.* 5. 1. 3 and 7.

[256] See Plotinus, *Enn.* 4. 3. 12-17, 24. Antony-Athanasius do not distinguish between the All-Soul and the individual souls, though in the doctrine of Plotinus both remain united to a certain extent (see Inge, *op. cit.* 213-21).

[257] The First Principle of Plotinus' Divine Triad, also called the 'One,' the 'Absolute,' etc.—For the present section, see also J. M. Colleran's Introductions to St. Augustine's *De quantitate animae* and *De magistro,* in the preceding volume of the series—ACW 9. 9 and 118-20.

[258] See Athanasius' discourse on Christ's death on the Cross, *De Incarn.* 19-25.

[259] Egyptian tutelar divinities whose cult also spread to the Greeks and Romans. Isis' wanderings began when her husband, Osiris, was murdered by his plotting brother Typhon and cast into the Nile. She finally found the corpse, only to be forced into another long search when Typhon discovered the body, dismembered it into fourteen parts, and scattered these to the four winds. She recovered thirteen parts, buried them at Philoe. Osiris then inhabited the sacred bull Apis, and his wanderings took place from the death of one bull to the reappearance or reincarnation of Apis in another. Cf. Plutarch, *De Iside et Osiride* 12 ff.; Athenagoras, *Leg.* 22; Firmicus Maternus, *De err. prof. rel.* 2; Augustine, *De civ. Dei* 18. 5 (where Osiris = Serapis); T. A. Brady, 'Isis' and 'Osiris,' OCD (1949) 459 f. and 628.

[260] Cronus (Saturn to the Romans) was one of the Titans. He rebelled against his father Uranus, mutilated him, and took the world dominion from him. In the course of time his father's curse was visited upon him. Fearing for his throne, he swallowed his own children as they were born—Hestia, Demeter, Hera, Hades, and Poseidon. Zeus alone escaped. When he had grown up, he forced his father to regurgitate his brothers and sisters, defeated him in the battle with the Titans, and banished him to Tartarus. Cf. the account in Hesiod, *Theog.* 164 ff., 453 ff., 666 ff.; also the sarcastic treatment of the myth by Tertullian, *Ad nat.* 2. 12; H. J. Rose, 'Kronos,' OCD (1949) 476.

[261] The frequent castigation by the early Christian writers of allegory as a rationalization of the ancient myths, shows how commonly it was resorted to as a last desperate effort to defend the pagan pantheon against unbelievers and scoffers. See Tatian 21. 6-9; Athenagoras, *Leg.* 22; Origen, *Cont. Cels.* 4. 38, 48; 5. 37; 6. 42; Ps.–Clement, *Recog.* 10. 29-36; Gregory of Nazianzus, *Orat.* 4. 115-7; Augustine, *De civ. Dei* 4. 10; 6. 8; and especially the acid critique by Arnobius, *Adv. nat.* 4. 32-45 (= ACW 8. 440-51). The allegorical treatment was applied particularly to Homer—cf. the work published in Greek by the Stoic Heraclitus (probably in the Augustan period): *Quaestiones Homericae*, also known as *Allegoriae Homericae*. On allegorization by the Stoics, cf. S. Angus, *The Religious Quests of the Graeco-Roman World* (New York 1929) 29.

[262] On the gods and goddesses mentioned here, see the articles by H. J. Rose in OCD 68 f. (Apollo), 104 f. (Artemis), 412 (Hephaestus), 412 f. (Hera), 666 (Persephone), 721 (Poseidon).

²⁶³ Δημιουργός, lit. 'one who works for the people' = 'craftsman.' The word is used regularly by the Gnostics ('Demiurge': cf. Irenaeus, *Adv. haer.*, *passim*) for the creator of the universe. It is also found once in the New Testament (Heb. 11. 10) and in the Apostolic Fathers (Clement of Rome 20. 11; 26. 1; 33. 2; 59. 2; *Ad Diogn.* 7. 2; 8. 7) to designate the Christian *opifex mundi*. See the note by Newman, *Select Treatises* 2. 400 f.

²⁶⁴ 'Religious truth' for τὸ μυστήριον of the text. The various meanings of this difficult term in the New Testament and in early Christian literature have evoked much profound study. The recent article by G. Bornkamm, TWNT 4 (1942) *s.v.*, 809-34, also considers the use of the term in the late fourth century (832); where see also the recent literature.

²⁶⁵ Literally, 'in the wisdom of Greek words'—see 1 Cor. 1. 17.

²⁶⁶ The text: εἰς Ἑλληνισμόν.

²⁶⁷ The word used here, δεισιδαιμονία, which to the pagan mind usually meant 'due respect to the gods' or simply 'religion,' but to the Christian became synonymous with 'superstition,' is undoubtedly a reminiscence of the same term used by St. Paul in addressing the philosophers at Athens, Acts 17. 22: 'Men of Athens, wherever I look I find you *scrupulously religious*' (δεισιδαιμονεστέρους —trans. by Knox). Cf. the study of P. J. Koets, Δεισιδαιμονία, *A Contribution to the Knowledge of the Religious Terminology in Greek* (Purmerend 1929).

²⁶⁸ With this and the following, compare *De Incarn.* 47; also Tertullian, *De idol.* 9; Ambrose, *Exam.* 4. 33.

²⁶⁹ Cf. also *De Incarn.* 48. Among numerous similar passages in the writings of the Fathers, Tertullian's *Semen est sanguis Christianorum* (*Apol.* 50. 6) has come down as one of antiquity's most celebrated aphorisms (cf. J. E. B. Mayor, *Q.Septimi Florentis Tertulliani Apologeticus* [Cambridge 1917] 482 f.); and Tertullian himself, so tradition has it, owed his conversion from a pagan lawyer and profligate, to his observation of the Christian men and women martyred in the Roman amphitheatre.

²⁷⁰ 1 Cor. 2. 4.

²⁷¹ Athanasius uses the imperfect ἔγραφον, implying repeated writing, as is also understood by Evagrius who adds the adverb *crebro*: they wrote to Antony 'repeatedly,' 'frequently.'

²⁷² See Heb. 1. 2.

²⁷³ These rulers had assured Antony that they worshipped

($\pi\rho o\sigma\kappa\upsilon\nu o\hat{\upsilon}\sigma\iota$) Christ. The emperors before Constantine had demanded worship for themselves. The refusal of emperor worship had been one of the main issues in the persecutions of the Christians. Here Antony reminds his imperial correspondents that they must not forget the Church's uncompromising position through the difficult times that lay behind: that all authority comes from God, that the one and true King and Emperor is Christ. Cf. the study by F. J. Dölger, 'Zur antiken und frühchristlichen Auffassung der Herrschergewalt von Gottes Gnaden,' *Ant. u. Christ.* 3 (1932) 117-127.

[274] See Dan. 4. 16.

[275] Serapion (or Sarapion) was a very common name in Egypt and in Egyptian monastic literature (Butler 2. 213 f.). The man mentioned here (see also below, § 91) had been superior of a colony of monks before he became bishop of Thmuis in Lower Egypt. Sozomen (*Hist. Eccl.* 4. 9) states that he was a man of extraordinary holiness and eloquence, and St. Jerome (*De vir. ill.* 99) speaks of his great learning. A friend of Athanasius, he suffered with him during the Arian disorders, was ousted from his see, for which he was known as 'confessor' in the orthodox Nicaean circles. He is also known for a work against the Manichaeans, and especially for his *Euchologium* or Sacramentary, a collection of thirty liturgical prayers, first published near the close of the last century and of capital importance for the history of the Church's early liturgy. Cf. Bardenhewer 3. 98-102; G. Bardy, 'Sérapion de Thmuis,' DTC 14. 2 (1941) 1908-12; for the *Euchologium*, J. Wordsworth, *Bishop Sarapion's Prayer-Book* (2nd ed. London 1923); also J. Quasten, *Monumenta eucharistica et liturgica vetustissima* (Bonn 1935) 49-67, with complete bibliography.

[276] For ἔνδον —cf. v. Hertling, op. cit. 75 n. 1.

[277] These troubles evidently were going on when St. Athanasius was composing the biography, for here he speaks of the '*present* assault of the Arians.' The biography is now quite generally assumed to have been set down in the year 357, after Athanasius had escaped an attack on his life (*De fuga* 24 f.) in February of the year before and fled to the monks in Upper Egypt (cf. Gregory of Nazianzus, *Orat.* 21. 19). In the apology for his flight, *De fuga* 3 f., 6 f., he describes the cruelties and excesses practiced by the Arians when the Church and orthodoxy seemed doomed (also the orthodox bishops in the West, including Pope Liberius, had been

deposed and banished after the synods of Arles in 353 and Milan in 355). Cf. Athanasius, *Hist. Ar.* 31 ff.

[278] The comparison, here and somewhat earlier, of the Arians with mules seems quite illustrative of Antony's homespun and unvarnished appraisal of persons and things; but the parallel drawn is also consistent with Athanasius' trenchant opinions about the Arians (see above, nn. 235 and 240). Regarding the 'senselessness' of the Arians (ἀλογία, which can also mean 'want of respect'), see Card. Newman's excellent note, ''Αλογία, ''Αλογος,' *Select Treatises* 2. 364 f.; to quote his introductory remark: 'This epithet is used by Athan. against the Arians, as if, by denying the eternity of the Logos (Reason or Word), first, they were denying the Intellectual nature of the Divine Essence; and, secondly, were forfeiting the source and channel of their own rational nature.'

[279] Matt. 17. 20 (Greek).

[280] John 16. 23 f.

[281] Matt. 10. 8.

[282] Matt. 7. 2.

[283] Δούξ, from the Latin *dux* (English 'duke'): during the later Roman imperial times, a military commander in a province. This office was created by Diocletian to weaken the power of the prefects who up to that time had held the civil power as well as the command of the troops stationed in a province. Cf. O. Seeck, 'Dux,' RE 5 (1905) 1869-75; also the material in Du Cange, *Gloss. graec. s.v.*, 327 f. and App. 61.

[284] Balacius was military commander *(dux)* in the province of Egypt from 340-345. Cf. O. Seeck, 'Balakius,' RE 5 (1905) 2816. Athanasius repeats the story of his death in *Hist. Ar.* 14.

[285] Cf. Athanasius, *Hist. Ar.* 12.

[286] Nestorius was prefect from 345 to 352; cf. W. Ensslin, 'Nestorius' no. 2, RE 17 (1937) 137.

[287] A town in Lower Egypt, approximately seventeen miles southeast of Alexandria. It was the last station on the roads leading from Memphis and Pelusium over Andropolis to Alexandria. It is known today as El Keriun. Cf. K. Sethe, 'Χαιρέου (πόλις),' RE 3 (1899) 2030.

[288] See above, n. 86.

[289] A metaphor from anointing athletes for the games of the Greeks and Romans. See in the *Passio SS. Perpetuae et Felicitatis* 10. 7, the vision of Perpetua in which she sees herself rubbed with

oil in preparation for her contest with the Devil, here called the Egyptian.

²⁹⁰ Cf. Matt. 27. 60 f.; Mark 15. 46.

²⁹¹ Christianity brought to Egypt a spiritualized view of the after-life, and, consequently, a decrease in concern for the body after death. Mummification, a practice which had sought the preservation of the body as a necessary partaker in the future life, was discontinued more and more. Cf. Mackean, *Christian Monasticism in Egypt* 58; H. Leclercq, 'Momie,' DACL 11. 2 (1934) 1744-52.

²⁹² The *Historia Lausiaca* (21) identifies these monks as Macarius and Amatas (cf. Butler's note, 2. 193 f.). See also Jerome, *Vita S. Pauli* 1, and *Chron. an.* 361.

²⁹³ Probably 3 Kings 2. 2 is referred to (cf. also Jos. 23. 14), though Daniel actually says: 'I am going the way of all the earth' (πάσης τῆς γῆς).

²⁹⁴ See above, § 19, where Antony explains in detail what 'dying daily' means. See also Jerome, *Epist.* 53. 10; 60.14; 127. 6.

²⁹⁵ See above, § 68 f.

²⁹⁶ Luke 16. 9.

²⁹⁷ Jerome in his legendary life of Paul of Thebes relates (12) that when Antony at the age of ninety visited the senior solitary who was then one hundred and thirteen, Paul requested him to return to his own cell and fetch the cloak presented to him by Athanasius and to bury him in it.

²⁹⁸ The grave was discovered in the year 561 and his body transferred to Alexandria. When the Saracens made themselves masters of Egypt in 635, the remains were brought to Constantinople. From there they came to France in the late tenth or early eleventh century, and since 1491 they have been kept in the Church of Saint Julien in Arles. Cf. R. Hindringer, 'Antonius, hl., Abt,' LTK 1 (1930) 514.

²⁹⁹ See above, § 10; v. Hertling, *op. cit.* 88.

³⁰⁰ See the Prologue.

INDEX